The Humor of Jesus

The Humor of Jesus:
Sources of Laughter in the Bible

EARL F. PALMER

REGENT COLLEGE PUBLISHING
• Vancouver, British Columbia •

Published 2001 by Regent College Publishing
an imprint of the Regent College Bookstore
5800 University Blvd., Vancouver, BC V6T 2E4 Canada
www.regentpublishing.com

The views expressed in works published by Regent College Publishing
are those of the author and may not necessarily represent
the official position of Regent College.

Printed on demand in the United States of America
The paper used in this publication
meets the minimum requirements of the
American National Standard for Information Sciences —
Permanence of Paper for Printed Library Materials, ANSI Z39.48-1984.

Canadian Cataloguing in Publication Data

Palmer, Earl F.
The Humor of Jesus

Includes bibliographical references.
ISBN 1-55361-015-6 (Canada)
ISBN 1-57383-180-8 (United States)

1. Wit and humor in the Bible.
2. Wit and humor – Religious aspects – Christianity. I. Title.
BS680.W63P34 2000   220.6   C00-911170-0

Contents

Preface

Earl F. Palmer

Why do people laugh? It might be a stand-up comedian who makes us laugh, or a book, or a film. Sometimes we laugh because a daily life experience strikes us as funny. Ordinary people with no training in showmanship make us laugh. Families laugh at a reunion picnic. Babies and their grandparents always make us laugh. Laughter is universal on earth and laughter even happens in heaven according to Jesus. He reminds us of that just after telling about 99 safe sheep and one that is found (Luke 15). But not all sources of laughter are as good as these; laughing is sometimes cruel; there is laughter that originates in the intention to harm, there is hysterical laughter that is chaotic, but even the laughter of despair does not cancel out the importance of good laughter.

This book is an exploration of the sources of laughter that are found in the biblical witness to the life and ministry of Jesus Christ. This exploration is important because laughter that has joy at its source is as vital to the health of the soul as it is for the health of the body.

I have wanted to publish this study of the humor of Jesus because, for as long as I can remember, I have been fascinated with all of the kinds of comedy. Most of my favorite stories were the ones that made me laugh— even if they also made me cry. Most of my favorite people have been the ones who have had a sense of humor. That started early for me with my mother, who had a marvelously dry wit. My father could not tell jokes, but he laughed enthusiastically at all the ones he heard and especially those told by his children. My own children are the funniest children I've ever met and their mother, my wife Shirley, is the best foil for every instance of family humor because of a certain innocent sincerity that means she rarely sees double meanings in jokes until we explain them, which makes everything all the more fun.

I have been fortunate to be a pastor in three congregations that each loved to laugh: University Presbyterian Church in Seattle, Washington; Union Church of Manila, Philippines; and First Presbyterian Church of Berkeley, Berkeley, California. I have been mentored in this subject throughout my life as a pastor by many people in these congregations who have encouraged me as their teacher and pastor to discover and share the rich sources of humor in the Bible.

I want to especially thank some of the people who have helped me with this book—four gifted people have helped me with my manuscript, Ms. Mary Bauer, Ms. Elizabeth Westburg, Ms. Suzanne Giannini and my wife Shirley.

This book is dedicated to some of the people of humor in my life:

My family

Shirley
Greg, Anne and Sarah
Jon, Kara Diane and Andrew
Eric, Elizabeth and Katherine and Peter

My two prayer groups

Bob

Bruce

Denny

Mas

Walt

Eric

Tim

John

Paul

Aaron

Todd

Jason

Ryan

Monson

Sid

Alan

The other funniest people in my life

Paul McKowen

Dick Jacobson

Donn Moomaw

Dale Bruner

Ted Nissen

Bob Deery

Dick Blomquist

Don Nielson

Hubie Newton

My Old Roommates

Lynn Boliek

Kayton Roy Palmer

Vince Mok

Dale Parker

Bill Hiedeger

*P.S. This book is about Humor and therefore
I think three top twelve lists make sense:*

The Twelve Funniest Writers I Have Read

Mark Twain
The Greatest American Comic Philosopher, both funny and wise.

C. S. Lewis
Brilliant at satire, analogy and the best letter writer I have read.

John Bunyan
A wit that is rich in understanding of the human personality
and the wonder of God's grace.

G.K. Chesterton
No one uses language better than G.K. Chesterton.

Dorothy Sayers
She has a bold edge to her descriptions, both funny and insightful.

Robert Benchley
The master of the humor of misunderstandings.

Patrick McManus
Totally off the wall and down to earth at the same time.

Garrison Keillor
A modern story-teller to match Mark Twain.

Dr. Seuss
Clever and funny and warm-hearted.

A. A. Milne
He knows how to create characters
in which we see ourselves and then laugh.

William Shakespeare
He understands how to mix humor and pathos.

Maurice Sendak
Is there any poem with as much fun and moral truth as "Pierre"?

The Twelve Funniest Comedians I Have Seen

Jonathan Winters
No one takes you on and surprises you like Winters.

Bob Hope
The master of stand-up comedy.

W.C. Fields
The bumbling put-down artist.

Lucille Ball
America's funniest woman.

Dick Van Dyke
He mixes a human touch with impishness.

Ray Goulding & Bob Elliott
These two always take you in and you know it's happening.

Red Skelton
America's clown with a warm and totally child-like heart.

Jack Benny
No one had timing down like Benny.

Mary Tyler Moore
You love her and want to laugh with her.

Bill Cosby
You feel he knows all about you.

Johnny Carson
The perfect interview master, especially with ordinary people

John Cleese
The Master of Misunderstanding

The Twelve Funniest Movies I Have Seen

Singing in the Rain
This film has charm, wit and superb dancing.

Wizard of Oz
An all time classic that helps us understand our deepest fears and hopes.

Good Morning Vietnam
Brilliant mix of comedy and heartbreak,
a film with no throw-away characters.

Mary Poppins
For the child of every age.

Road to Rio
Bob Hope and Bing Crosby at their best.

Around The World in 80 Days
The cameo scenes are the best of any film.

The Bank Dick
Wacky and just plain funny.

It's a Mad, Mad, Mad, Mad World
Worth the price for one scene with Jonathan Winters.

A Night at the Opera
The Marx Brothers classic – set a standard for slapstick.

Yankee Doodle Dandy
Who could have thought Cagney could dance?

What's Up Doc?
Improbable story, totally fun.

Strictly Ballroom
A sleeper film in which every character surprises you.

"I've often thought that the gigantic secret of God is mirth."
G.K. Chesteron

Chapter One

Humor

There is a surprise at the center of everything that is funny. President Reagan during a presidential visit to the People's Republic of China was shown the famous archeological site of the one thousand terra-cotta soldiersby his host, the paramount leader, Deng Xian Peng. The President stood at the viewing platform and expressed respectful amazement to his hosts, but the comedian in Ronald Reagan could not resist a humorous possibility in the presence of the great antiquity they were all viewing. The President called out to the stone soldiers, "At ease!" While some local humor is trapped by ethnic experience and understanding, this command was immediately understood by both the Chinese hosts and the American visitors who all laughed heartily. Here were soldiers permanently frozen at attention; Ronald Reagan thought it was time to give them a rest.

Humor has many faces but the element of surprise is always there. What is funny may be uncomplicated like "At ease!" or there may echo within a funny sentence more profound themes. Fatigue and disappointment are sometimes the sources of the humorous possibility that is able to make us laugh even at what we fear or what we resent.

Bob Hope entertained American fighting men and women in every war that America faced from World War II to Desert Storm. One Christmas Bob Hope entertained American forces in Da Nang, Vietnam, during the Vietnam War. One of his funniest one-line jokes, and one that received the biggest laugh from his vast crowd of American soldiers was when he said to the young men and women in front of his makeshift stage, "I just want you to know that your country back home is 50 percent behind you with our support." In this case, the comedian philosopher, Bob Hope told his audience what was for them a bitter truth, but it took his listeners by surprise and was very funny precisely because it was the harsh truth they all knew, but Bob Hope the master storyteller had fooled them when he sprang it upon them. They had all expected to hear one more empty platitude of support from the home front that would not have been empty in an earlier war, but was now in this unpopular war. He started his sentence in the direction that we would have expected but when the surprise came they knew that the comedian Bob Hope understood their feelings, their grief, their resentment, their homesick fatigue. He had connected with them at a deeper level with that one line joke and it worked as humor because they knew where he stood among Americans back home. It was Christmas and the great humorist was standing there among his young friends on a field in Vietnam and it gave him the right to tell the truth to surprise his audience with the truth. A draft evader could not have told this joke. In a subtle and wise way, Bob Hope also helped his young audience to disarm some of the toxic side effects of the truth in his joke. This is the healing effect of good humor.

Humor is more complicated than laughter because of the source of the surprise and because of the differences in the mandate that is the motivation for each humorist. The sources of humor differ from person to person and situation to situation. It is clear that President Reagan's mandate at the moment of "At ease!" is a different one than what Bob Hope faced in Da Nang.

What then are some of those differences in the kinds of humor? And how do they fit together to enrich human experience with the gift of laughter? The most common form of humor is the surprise of initial confusion or misinformation which, when it is later clarified, the humor in it breaks in upon us. Big Bird in Sesame Street sings a song about the biggest word he has ever seen—"It starts off like an 'a' word as any one can see but then in the middle it gets awfully queer to me . . ." Later we realize that Big Bird has seen the alphabet which he misunderstood as a very long word. When the misunderstanding dawns upon us we see the humor in his mistake. In this form of humor the joke is on the teller and it depends on a flaw or an incompleteness in the teller's understanding. We are laughing at our own human inadequacy.

Another form of the humor of human frailty finds its linkage to the fears of normal people. One of the funniest scenes in all of literature is the raft incident in *Huckleberry Finn,* during which a boat approaches the raft on which Huck and his companion (the runaway slave, Jim) are hiding. The men in the boat shout at they see Huck, "Hey boy, have you seen a runaway slave?" Huck who is experienced at telling lies shouts back, "Come please and help us. My pappy is sick with the small pox. Please come help us!" The men paddle quickly away and leave Huck and Jim alone. Mark Twain has humorously shown that the reality of fear will overpower other motives in the lives of most human beings, and has absolute sway over those rough men who are hunting for bounty!

Another form of humor is the surprise of grace when the laughter comes from the discovery of something so good it takes us by surprise. Lloyd Alexander's great stories, *The Book of Three,* has just such a surprise at its best part. The young assistant pig keeper, Taran, is told by a wise sage that when he looks into a magic pool he will see the prince's face. Therefore the young man Taran searches for the magic pool as a grand and supreme moment for his quest. To his surprise, when he finally looks into the pool, he sees the reflection of his own face. Unknown to him, because he only saw himself as an assistant pig keeper, the fact all along is that Taran is the prince of the kingdom and when the time was right he was meant to discover that good fact.

Another form of humor is the humor of justice which occupies a very major part in every adventure story. The triumph of truth over falsehood will usually combine both the shout of cheer at the victory of truth, but also the laughter of enjoyment at the moment of realization when the evil that early in the story appeared so overwhelming and invincible now is seen in comic relief as totally overrated and inflated when compared to the greater staying power of goodness. This is the final joy and celebration in the story of Snow White when the apparently fatal curse of the queen/witch, which had its power because of envy and selfishness, is overcome by the faithfulness of Snow White's small friends and the kiss of a prince who loved her. Justice has its laughter because of the surprise of its victory over evil.

Ironic humor is well understood. It is the surprise of laughter that comes because things are not as they appear to be. Something or some person may appear weak, but then later on as the story unfolds what seemed weak at one point in the story turns out to be strong. At the moment of that new discovery, the irony of contrast between appearance and reality is the source of an ironic humor. In the film, *Bad Day at Black Rock*, Spencer Tracy plays the part of a man who stops for a two-day visit in a small desert town to inquire about an old war time friend of his. Soon we realize that he has stumbled upon a dark and evil secret of murder in the small town. The character Tracy plays seems weak because of a war injury so that he only has the use of one arm but ironically, he has the inner righteous power of his quest for truth and in addition to that moral power during a hotel bar room fight, he proves to have the skill of karate. The film is dark, but the humor is evident in the ironic surprises of both his formidable character and his karate skill. Every film audience laughs with relief at the bar room fight sequence. The ironic humor is in the contrast of one sane and courageous man in the small town of confused and frightened small people caught up in the insanity of prejudice and fear.

The simplest of all forms of humor are dual surprises of the interruption of the unexpected, and its opposite, the persistence of repetition. Both of these sources of laughter work well together and they have always been the specialty of children. Children love to see things repeated and in the repetition we find ourselves laughing. Children also love to meet up with a good surprise of the unexpected; therefore the good shock of the unexpected appearance of a friendly monster makes us laugh. Family cultural traditions combine these two forms of humor in the way birthdays are observed and the way presents are given on Christmas morning. Jack Benny was the master of repetitious humor—so much so that in his radio comedy hour an audience of faithful listeners would laugh every time a reference was made to his tight-fisted ways with money. In one famous scene, a would-be hold up man comes up behind Jack Benny and points a gun at Benny and gruffly demands "Your money or your life." There is a long pause and finally the would-be robber Mel Blanc with one of his character voices speaks again, "Did you hear me old man, I said, Your money or your life." Again a pause and finally Benny says, "I'm thinking. I'm thinking." This is the humor of repetition because everyone knows Mr. Benny well enough to enjoy the problematic decision he faces. We expected it; yet we laughed when it happened. We also recognize one of the many voices of Mel Blanc as the voice of the robber and that increases the sense of repetitious comedy that was the trademark specialty of the Jack Benny show.

In the same way Jerry Seinfeld only needed to say "Hello Newman" and his loyal audience would roar with laughter. If repetition is humorous it is also true that the shock of the unexpected is what provides the comic energy in slapstick. The Marx Brothers pressed this form of comedy to its classic summit. In one scene Harpo Marx, who does not speak, is leaning against a wall. Someone walks by and asks him in a derisive way "What are you doing here, stupid? Are you holding up the wall?" Harpo nods eagerly in agreement. Two others come by and ask the same question and he nods again as they laugh and remark how stupid he appears. At that point, Harpo Marx walks away and the whole wall falls to the ground. This is the wonderful slapstick humor of the improbable and the unexpected.

Chapter 2
The Many Faces of Humor

Not all humor is nourishing to the soul or "just plain fun." Everyone who has been the target of cruelty disguised as a joke knows this. There is humor that has as its starting point the sourness of cynicism. The surprise element may still be present but after a while the laughter of cynicism thins to the predictability of flippancy. Few writers interpret this arid condition more accurately than C. S. Lewis in his *Screwtape Letters*. His chapter on the sources of laughter describes flippancy as a form of humor that creates an armor plating against both God and humanity. He writes, "Among flippant people the joke is always assumed to have been made . . . every serious subject is treated as if they have already found the ridiculous side to it . . . and it excites no affection among those who practice it."[1]

What is the purpose and meaning of humor? *Healthy* humor connects human beings and creates self-understanding. The humor of cynicism is one of the markers of despair and it has that effect upon those who practice

1. C. S. Lewis, *The Screwtape Letters* (London: Fount, 1955) p. 60.

it. There is a mockery at the core of the jokes of despair whether they are about sex or race or religion or politics. They tear at the value and perceived worth of whatever person or aspect of life that is the object of the joke. Such humor is used by the storyteller to spread emptiness and to create a special kind of collaboration with listeners that destroys shame and guilt through the mockery at the core of the humorous surprise in the joke or story. The result in the jokes of mockery is that the object of the story sentence or comic statement is isolated and separated from the one who tells the story with the result that moral obligation toward that person is cancelled and emptied by the humor. Racist jokes are told for this very reason and become therefore a preliminary step toward the justification of cruelty toward a person who has now been objectified and humorously depersonalized. The humor of despair may then become the humor of anger and finally the humor of harm. The role of humor in this case is to diminish worth through ridicule and once that emptying has happened a climate of permission to do harm is put into place. This is the essence of the comedy of the Master of Ceremonies in the important but troubling musical *Cabaret*. Each story and song by the Cabaret Master of Ceremonies is carefully targeted against some person or group and is designed to destroy their worth and significance. The musical which is set in the Berlin of the early 1930s shows how educated people could be coaxed toward the horrors of the anti-semitism of Nazism—and laugh all the way. The Master of Ceremonies leads his audience with his dagger-like humor of evil toward a place where those whose life is in the cabaret feel the permission to do harm toward those who have become the object of the jokes.

Joseph Conrad creates two characters in his novel *Victory* that are expert at the humor of despair and he shows how powerful such humor is in spreading terror. Two mysterious Englishmen with their Colombian alligator-hunter manservant arrive in a south Asian port city; they are total enigmas to the German hotel keeper who houses most European visitors in the seedy port town. They appear as comic characters from their earliest description by Conrad. The one at check-in gives as his name to the manager of the hotel the name "plain Mr. Jones" and his secretary is "Ricardo." The powerful manservant is "Pedro," who stays in the town but is clearly the obedient servant of the two. The German hotel keeper is suspicious of his guests from the beginning, but his suspicions turn to over-whelming fear as the two mystery guests humorously tell of how easy it has been for them to kill the people who stand in their way. Their most humor-ous story is that of the killing in the Colombian jungle of their manservant's brother, which they explain to the hotel manager as the reason why Pedro is now so totally devoted to them: "'Shall I tell you how I killed his brother in the wilds of Columbia? Well, perhaps some other time—it's a rather long story. What I shall always regret is that I didn't kill him too. I could have done it without extra trouble then; now it's too late. Great nuisance; but he's useful sometimes."[2] The offhand, hard manner and contemptuous tone of "plain Mr. Jones" disconcerted Schomberg utterly. This uneasiness was caused by the humor of cruelty and would later turn into sheer terror for Schomberg, even though he himself was already a cruel man before his guests had arrived.

Threatening sources of laughter create at first low grade and later on intense fear because we who experience such laughter sense the chaos that exists just over the edge of that boundary that marks the difference between the meaning of life and living beings over against the lack of significance for life and living beings. We who laugh at such stories have drifted over that significance boundary line and it gradually dawns on us that the laughter that greets us there is the laughter of chaos.

Drunkenness, like certain forms of insanity, also produces laughter that is lacking in significance and therefore produces its own kind of disturbing chaos. It is laughter without a reason, except that the restraints on emotion and cultural inhibition have been blurred or removed. Such laughter creates no memories of well-being, as every child who has endured the raucous laughter of a drunk father on Christmas Eve knows. The laughter of alco-hol or drugs is a thousand miles away from fun or celebration, and no drunk father or mother is able to assure a child of their own special worth. A slurred "I love you" is hollow and we know it, just as the running laughter because of chemical imbalance produces fatigue and never interpersonal energy.

But there is good laughter and it has an altogether different result. The laughter that nourishes has the opposite result because at its motivational center the humorist has recognized a connectedness toward those who surround his or her story so that the goal is to connect us and not to disengage us from that human linkage. Nourishing humor intends to build up and not to tear apart the sense of well-being of the object of the humorous story. This nourishing goal is present even in the revelatory aspect of every joke that exposes weaknesses or fears in the object or subject of a story. Our pride is always embarrassed by a humorous anecdote, but the result is nevertheless healthy if I was able to learn about myself from the humorous story. Humor by its surprise of laughter takes the harsh sting out of self exposure. I actually welcome the new self-understanding of my fears or frailty which in a more didactic setting of direct statement of fact I would oppose and seek to deflect toward those around me. The laughter from good humor makes it possible for the person with resentments to disarm and realistically reassess some of the most bitter edges of those resentments. In all of this for those who suffer real harm such as prejudice or injustice a remarkable kind of equilibrium is achieved that rebalances a man or woman away from the possibility of self pity of the victim mentality toward a more healthy self understanding. Humor levels the ground between the kinds of power that people make use of to find their way and to get their way.

But best of all we need to laugh because life is exciting and the source of happiness is as joyous as it is serious. We need to laugh because people matter. We need to laugh because people can be hurt by what happens while living and always need to find their balance, to steady their perspectives realistically and to keep their sense of humor. Laughter helps all of these things to happen.

We need to laugh because the best surprise of all is that there is laughter in Heaven. Jesus himself, said so (Luke 15).

Chapter Three

Jesus the Humorist

Jesus of Nazareth is the greatest humorist of all time for three reasons: First, because of the breadth of what he knows about reality. The best humorists always understand what is going on, and better than others do. Secondly, Jesus is good to the core and the greatest humor has always had its source in the good surprise of grace. St. Paul said it well in his very best and profoundly humorous one line summary of the meaning of the life, death and victory of Jesus: "Where sin increased the grace of God increased more" (Rom 5). We have always thought evil was so strong and we therefore have always feared evil, but in fact the love of God revealed in the beloved son, Jesus Christ can outdistance every sin, human or cosmic, every time. The third reason will itself take us by surprise. Jesus is the greatest humorist because he is the most *normal* man we have ever met. It is a fact that the best comedy does not come from the strange words of confusion but from the clear headed words of a clear vision of reality. Confusion, whether it is cruel or drugged or silly is not really funny in the same robust way as is the humor of clearheadedness.

Lily Tomlin is funny because she is quick witted and thinks well on her feet. She creates characters such as Ernestine that may seem dimwitted but Lily Tomlin is not dimwitted. Her show, "Is There Intelligent life on Earth?" proves the point and answers her question. Yes, Lily is clear headed and indeed intelligent.

Jesus is decidedly not like the people around him in the Mediterranean world of the first century, and yet he is able to identify with all of them and at the same time stay understandable. We are able to sketch in the atmosphere of the first century world with discovered archeological evidence and ancient documents so that we can understand the major human players of the time of Jesus. As we better understand who they were we can then better understand how remarkable Jesus is as he stands among them.

The story of Israel as the people of God has a complicated and most of the time unhappy history for the one thousand years following King David (1000 B.C.). King David had been the one obvious success of the Jewish story. His son, Solomon, shared that same cultural and political success, but following the death of Solomon civil war between the North and South wiped out most of the glory. Soon the greater world powers around the people of Israel would totally dominate its history but not crush its spirit. The years after Solomon are hard years. The attack of the Assyrian Empire in 720 B.C. destroyed the Northern Empire and the attack of the NeoBabylonian Empire in 586 B.C. would destroy Jerusalem and take the remaining population, the Southern Kingdom, to Babylon as captives. Through this period the Jewish prophets wrote and spoke of the hope that God would not forget the promise He made to Israel's founders, Abraham and Sarah. The most dramatic part of Israel's story is not the heroic story of battles won but the fact of its very survival against heavy odds and the survival of its poetry and its profound hope. Finally, with the Persian Empire's rise and defeat of ancient Babylon the remnant of the Jews are brought back to Jerusalem and once again they try to rebuild their city along with their ancient Abrahamic and Davidic hopes.

Alexander the Great swept the ancient world in 336 B.C. and brought with his military victories Greek culture and language to the Middle East. It is because of this Hellenization of the ancient world that the Old

Testament was translated into Greek at 100 B.C. (the Septuagint) and that our New Testament was written in Greek. At Alexander's death his generals divided what now remained of his empire. The Jews and their land then suffered under one of Alexander's generals, the cruel despot Seleucid I, and finally Antiochos Seleucid. A change in this tyranny happened in 150 B.C. when a family of brothers called the Maccabeans led a Jewish revolt against the Seleucids. This revolt was successful for the Jewish patriots because on the western front of the Seleucid empire a new world power was putting pressure on the Seleucids, a world power that would finally end their rule—the Romans. The lull that resulted in world politics enabled the Hasmonean house of the Maccabeans to establish their family reign in Judah for almost one hundred years until the conquering armies of Rome were to gain control of the whole of the Mediterranean world from Europe to Egypt in 80 B.C.

This 150 year period of time just before the beginning of the Christian era is very important for us to understand if we are to make sense of the people who lived as contemporaries of Jesus of Nazareth. Who are they and what are they like?

The ones who controlled and served the institution of the high priesthood of the temple were able in this period of time to consolidate their authority over the official religion of Israel with its Sanhedrin Council. This group became major actors in the New Testament narratives. They are called the Sadducees.

A very important lay movement begins at about 160 B.C., first as brave freedom fighters with the Judas Maccabean family and later as a lay movement that becomes critical of the corruption of the Hasmonean family once their military victory had secured their power. This movement had two parties. The one more hard line under Rabbi Shammai and the other under Rabbi Hillel more moderate. This movement of devout laymen called themselves the Pharisees, "the separate ones."

The Hasmonean house itself reigns for about one hundred years but at the time just prior to the first century, two final male heirs become ineffective in their leadership which enable a Nabatean citizen named Antipater who was prime minister to the final Hasmonean king to become the de facto power behind the king. Antipater was a shrewd man who correctly read the political script of this fast moving time of change in the fortunes of nations and decided to favor two young Roman generals, Mark Antony and Octavian, over against their seleucid, Egyptian and Persian foes. These Roman officers in appreciation for his support recommended to Julius Caesar and obtained for Antipater the gift of Roman citizenship as well as ore mines that he was permitted to exploit tax free. Antipater sent his younger son to Rome to study and at his own death by assassination this son of Antipater was named King of the Jews by his father's old friend Octavian's recommendation to Julius Caesar. Later this young officer Octavian would rule the Roman empire under the name of Caesar Augustus. It was Roman policy to put in place local kings in the territories they controlled as a technique of governance. This son of Antipater was Herod and he became known as Herod the Great. He was king for 33 years until 4 B.C. In an attempt to legitimize his kingship among the Jewish people, Herod divorced his wife Doris and married the last heir of the famous Maccabean family. Her name was Mariamne. Later he became suspicious of Mariamne and murdered her as well as two of his children by her. This is the Herod who built the temple of Jerusalem and who the wise men asked about a king born to the Jews. At Herod's death in 4 B.C. his son, Herod Antipas (4 B.C.–A.D. 39) became king. This is the Herod that was confronted by John the Baptist. Herod Antipas reigned during the ministry of Jesus. He was as brutal and as rich as his father. He benefited from the financial benefits that the Romans had given to his grandfather and father and was able as his father did to build lavish castles and seaside villas as well as aqueduct systems. It was he who finished the building of the temple in Jerusalem.

The Essenes, a group of religious and social separatists who isolated themselves from the life of the people of Israel, also made up a part of the puzzle of the people of the first century story. There were two distinct groups of Essenes, the one group which rejected marriage and lived as a secluded male community; the other group was not as strict and accepted marriage but still followed a strict and uncompromising code. This second group lived in Qumran near the Dead Sea and what has been fortunate for biblical scholars and archeologists is that the people in this Qumran community were careful librarians who stored in some 26 caves a vast collection of documents that were first discovered in 1946. These caves that overlook the Dead Sea have provided scholars of the Bible with complete copies and commentaries on all the books of the Old Testament except for Esther. The Essene manuals of discipline and special prayers have given us a fascinating window into the period just before the beginning of the first century A.D.

At the time of Jesus there were also Zealots—fierce opponents of the Roman occupation of the land of the Jews. These patriot terrorists unrealistically and tragically underestimated the power and tenacity of the Roman Empire's rule. Roman policy was clear and unequivocal on one point and that was that nothing would be permitted to defy the reign of the peace of Rome in any province of the empire. The Zealots and the population of the city of Jerusalem would pay a heavy price for this misunderstanding. Josephus, the pro-Roman Jewish historian of the later first century who would chronicle this whole period in his book, *The Jewish Wars*, would actually blame the destruction of Jerusalem in A.D. 70 and the siege and fall of Masada (one of Herod's palaces that had been occupied by Jewish patriots) not so much on the severity of the Roman government as on the arrogance and terrorism of the Zealot party.

So during the New Testament story of Jesus of Nazareth, the Romans are there too! The Roman governor during the ministry of Jesus is Pontius Pilate (A.D. 26-36), who had a very uneven career as Procurator. He must live in rented quarters both at Caesarea on the Mediterranean Sea and in Jerusalem, and in both instances he is indebted to Herod Antipas who is the wealthy owner of both of these palaces. The one house Herod built and then named in honor of Mark Antony and therefore this house is called the Antonia Fortress in Jerusalem. Another grand villa he built and named for Caesar Augustus—the villa called Caesarea on the Mediterranean. Herod knew each Roman emperor as a friend whereas Pilate served Caesar as a bureaucrat. This made Pontius Pilate a very uneasy and fragile Roman Governor.

Jesus comes into this historical context of real people in real places and our first meeting of this Son of Man/Son of God at the beginning of his ministry is at the River Jordan. The intense firebrand prophet, John the Baptist, is there and Jesus asks John to baptize him. John the Baptist does not approve of this request by Jesus but nevertheless he does baptize Jesus. Following that baptism a miraculous sign is given by God to honor Jesus. A voice breaks in upon this scene of this sign of the humility of Jesus: "This is my beloved son in whom I am well pleased."

Jesus pleased his Father and he called upon a band of men and women to follow him. The challenge of Jesus to follow him was difficult for his first century followers, just as the challenge is difficult for those who follow him now, nevertheless it is true that Jesus pleased his disciples then and he pleases us too. To be around or near him is to become aware of our own brokenness in painful shocks of awareness like lightning bolts that streak into our consciousness. Nevertheless we still want to be as near to him as we can because he pleases us. We can not dismiss the man Jesus once we have even superficially noticed who he is. Jesus of Nazareth stands out and holds our attention at the deepest level not because Jesus is odd and eccentric but because Jesus is so normal in contrast to all who surround him. We are more peculiar than he is; he stays young and fresh with an enthusiasm for life that is healthy and spontaneous but we are the tired out ones who have made our faces and personalities twisted by cynicism. G.K. Chesterton expressed this remarkable wonder about the healthiness of God: "It is we who have sinned and grown old; our father is younger than we are."

Jesus Christ is the normal one and he is the one who therefore pleases us. Everyone else around him is quite odd by contrast. The House of Herod is the house of murderous intrigue; certainly Herod's family is the original dysfunctional family of all dysfunctional families. The Sadducee Party of the religious priesthood with Caiaphas and his father-in-law Annas have made religious hypocrisy such a practiced art that their every sentence is a double meaning sentence. Their questions are always the trick questions of entrapment. How can anyone carry on any dialogue with the Sadducees? The Pharisees have given up trying to dialogue with the Sadducees. The Essenes will not attend the temple because the Sadducees control the temple. The Zealots are terrorists who stir up riots. Who can enjoy being around a terrorist? They hide daggers under their clothes and live like tightly coiled springs. It is impossible to relax around a terrorist because they have their eyes always over your shoulder looking either for a signal to revolutionary action or for an anti-terrorist police operative to walk through the door. The Essenes are certainly interesting but they are weird by any standard and they don't bow to any common sense rules of reasonable behavior. Though they live in the desert they refuse to bathe or use any oils on their skin because they believe that "God loves rough skin."

What about the Romans who rule the land? They are intoxicated with power which always harms interpersonal relationships. The Romans assigned to Palestine are resentful at this assignment they have in Judea, such a forgotten and despised province, and among such a restless people. A Roman official knows that being put in the land of the Jews is not the sign of a leader on the way up the ladder of career development.

The groups we admire the most of all are the Pharisees and they take the most interest in Jesus. They argue with him and invite him into their houses. Jesus bothers them but they really care about listening to what he says. But the Pharisees are infected with self-righteousness and the arrogance of the narrowness of their convictions, they lack generosity of spirit. This combination makes them hard to be with for very long. They wear you out with their long list of the things they resent and the people that they disapprove of.

Jesus is the most normal man of all and he is the Son of God! He really is the whole and healthy man, the Son of Man, and he is well pleasing to us as well as to God. Jesus has about him the narrowness of truth in his clear centeredness but there is a liberating generosity about that narrowness that comes out in the deeds, the teachings, the conversations and the humor of Jesus. He pleases the people and that public affection for him lasts until the first day of Holy Week, Palm Sunday.

The great stain that all humanity must bear is how we in the human family would in that one terrifying week agree to destroy such a man as this one who fulfills the yearnings throughout the Old Testament for goodness and faithfulness (Ps 100). This longing of the Psalm 100 is our yearning, to find love and to find truth; the Old Testament song writers and prophets gave us words for that expectation, "Ho, everyone who thirsts come to the water . . . without money . . ." (Isa 62). Jesus pleases us because we see that these two hopes of ours come together in him. "The law came through Moses but grace and truth came in Jesus Christ God's son" (Jn 1).

The tragedy of Holy Week is that an odd coalition of unlikely people who each lived from different motives will come together to put down Jesus of Nazareth. A resonance of fear created a fearful theme that in the swift moving events of that short week convinced the key leaders of the people to destroy this normal man. Jesus, because of the sheer force of who he is, what he says, and what he does brings into question and creates uneasiness in each of us about ourselves. It came down to one question about this man, Jesus: Is this Jesus the true center point? We either must live from that center point or we ourselves will chose some other center or finally become the centerpoint ourselves (Bonhoeffer). The horror of the week that we call Holy Week is that on Thursday night through Friday we decided to abandon and to punish that true center.

The supreme surprise of Holy Week is that God allowed this inevitable arrogance on our part to take its fatal course. Human wrath and hurtfulness which is born either in the soul of despair or of pride can only be defeated by being absorbed and taken to its full limit. Jesus the normal man is the one who took that cup of deadly harm into his hands. "No one takes my life from me, I lay it down by my own authority. I have authority to lay it down and I have authority to take it again" (Jn 10). Bad Friday becomes Good Friday because of this very fact. It is Jesus of Nazareth who takes upon himself, at his own death on the cross, human sin and fear; Jesus at the cross disarms the power of cosmic evil itself (the Devil); and at the cross Jesus disarms the powers of death. At the cross they are defeated because their power is absorbed. Jesus does it and it is the cross that grants our forgiveness. All of our sins, the weak ones like fear and the cruel ones like wickedness are taken by Jesus. He alone absorbs their fury. He does what no one else can do. This is why we cannot confer forgiveness from our own resources upon anyone else or ourselves. We can not fully forgive because we cannot absorb the harm. But Jesus can and he did, therefore, the forgiveness we are able to show toward others is borrowed from him—forgiveness like love flows through us toward others because Christ forgives.

We can understand the laughter on the first day of the week when the profound victory of the cross is validated for the eleven exhausted and confused disciples. These men and the larger group of men and women who surround them feel an emptiness early on Easter morning. The mixture of all of their bad feelings; of guilt, regret, grief, anger, fear, loss of dreams, even the feeling of unfinished obligation to properly attend to the burial of their slain friend; with all of these depressing feelings the women go to the borrowed tomb of Jesus and it is their discovery on that morning that has caused Christians to worship each week on the first day of the week and celebrate the triumph of what we always yearned for: the triumph of goodness and faithfulness, love and truth. "They were glad when they saw the Lord" (Jn 20). They laughed the laughter of joy that day and started to write the songs of Christmas and Easter that we still sing. But they laughed and they proved an ancient adage: "He who laughs last, laughs best."

Chapter Four

The Source of Humor

Saint Paul calls upon believers in Jesus Christ to "abide in faith, hope and love" (1 Cor 13). He also says that of these three the greatest is love. Paul's argument in this passage is that these three virtues of Christian discipleship do not exist in dependence upon our feelings about them. If feelings control and determine these three it would mean that we have faith when we now feel faithful or hope when we feel optimistic about the future or love when our hearts are moved. But Saint Paul has a larger vision than that. He tells the Corinthians that love is stronger than feelings, stronger than even the tongues of men and angels that might inspire us. At some future but inescapable moment mystical language will fall silent, but love stays, "it never ends." Faith wagers on God's faithfulness in spite of the contradictions of our feelings. Hope, even in times when people are in dread about the future, continues to offer energy from the future certainty of Christ's triumph into the present world of our daily lives. For Paul, we hold to faith, hope and love in the very face of the enigma of the mirror we must look into: "We now see in the mirror an enigma." Faith, hope and love are the three grand words of Christian discipleship and they are not determined nor are they defined by our experience though we have strong experiences of faith, hope and love. But there is a word in the vocabulary of Christian discipleship that is filled with emotion and feeling from top to bottom and that word is "joy."

How do we understand this word within its New Testament setting? As with all of the words that appear in any set of narratives and letters such as the New Testament the first rule for interpretation is to watch the word in its use by the speakers and writers; watch the word as it is defined by usage in the texts themselves.

James, who is the bishop of the church in Jerusalem, writes a brief and practical book of advice to the early church. James who lives in a time of intense and growing persecution in Jerusalem makes a decisive use of the word joy. "Count it all joy, my brothers and sisters, when you meet trials because through the trials you will discover that God's faithfulness endures and the result as this faithfulness works itself out in our lives has a healthy effect as we experience that enduring steadfastness of God's good will for us" (Jas 1). What James is saying is that joy is the experience we have once we discover that in spite of the stresses of trials such as hardship and persecutions the faithfulness of God still outlasts the trials. When that endurance of discipleship is validated to a man or woman right in the middle of the perils and trials of living at a time even of persecution then the result is joy. At a physical level of human experience it is something like the joy a mountaineer feels once he or she is safely down the mountain after a successful summit climb. It is the joy of tested and validated endurance in the face of real odds. James is telling of the joy born in the proof that comes through testing.

Another New Testament text where the word joy appears is during the Thursday evening discourse of Jesus (Jn 13-16). Jesus shares with his disciples on that unforgettable evening his own promises to them of the Holy Spirit, as the one who will be their companion; Jesus calls them to the way of love and he prepares them for the lonely journey that he alone must take later in that night and the next day. In what he says he makes use of the word joy. Notice John 15:11, 20, 16: 20-24:

I have said these things to you so that my joy may be in

you, and that your joy may be complete . . . Remember the word that I said to you, 'Servants are not greater than their master.' If they persecuted me, they will persecute you; if they kept my word, they will keep yours also . . . Very truly, I tell you, you will weep and mourn, but the world will rejoice; you will have pain, but your pain will turn into joy. When a woman is in labor, she has pain, because her hour has come. But when her child is born, she no longer remembers the anguish because of the joy of having brought a human being into the world. So you have pain now; but I will see you again, and your hearers will rejoice, and no one will take your joy from you. On that day you will ask nothing of me, Very truly, I tell you, if you ask anything of the Father in my name, he will give it to you. Until now you have not asked for anything in my name. Ask and you will receive, so that your joy my be complete.

In this instance the source of joy is not our endurance because of God's grace at work in us but it is the validation of Christ himself and his victory that turns our sorrow into celebration. "Your sorrow will be turned to joy." Jesus compares this joy to the birth of a child that follows the intense suffering of a mother during the painful labor of childbirth itself. A brand new reality has taken place; new life has broken through much like the newness of childbirth but this new life is the reason for the joy that is able to put aside the grief of the Friday of Jesus Christ's suffering because of the victory of Easter Sunday.

Saint Paul also uses the word joy in a decisive way at the close of his letter to the Philippians:

Therefore, my brothers and sisters, whom I love and long for, my joy and crown, stand firm in the Lord in this way, my beloved . . . Rejoice in the Lord always; again I say, Rejoice. Let your gentleness be known to everyone. The Lord is near. Do not worry about anything, but in everything by prayer and supplication with thanksgiving let your requests be made know to God. And the peace of Lord, which surpasses all understanding, will guard your hearts and your minds in Christ Jesus.

Paul's encouragement to the Philippians is that they need to rejoice; he calls upon them to become moderate, unflappable, mellow (*epikos* means gentle, moderate), because the Lord is nearby. If Jesus is alongside then why should the Philippians panic? Paul's affirmation is clear; we are able to relax in the best sense of the word when we are assured of the companionship of Jesus Christ the Lord. In this text the word joy has the peaceful and quiet meaning of "well being" that comes from the living presence of Christ as our present and real friend the one who is near to us and who by his peace guards our souls.

In each of these texts the Greek word for joy that is used is *chara*. This word has as its core meaning "surprise" as experienced in a positive and expansive sense. This word becomes the root word for the word especially used by Paul as a part of his love vocabulary, and that word *charis* is the word we know in the English text as "grace." Grace is surprise gift love for Paul. The long form of this word *charismata* is the word translated "gift" as in 1 Corinthians 12, where Paul tells of the gifts of the Holy Spirit. When the Greek prefix *eu* is placed before *charis* we have the very important New Testament word *eucharist* which means "thanksgiving": the good surprise gift given to someone or to God is what we call the gratitude of thanksgiving. These words are each in their own way vital words in the vocabulary of Christian faith. They are Greek words and they have their counterparts in the Hebrew and Aramaic language systems of the first century too.

From the time of Alexander the Great forward (33 B.C.) the Greek language increasingly become the universally understood language of the Mediterranean world even for the Jews. This is the reason that in 100 B.C. the Rabbis of Jerusalem commissioned 70 Rabbis to prepare in Alexandria, Egypt, a complete Greek text of the sacred scriptures; this document is called the "Septuagint" (usually abbreviated with roman numerals for 70, "LXX"). Most Jews of the first century would have read the Old Testament scriptures in this Greek language text. Jesus probably spoke most of his teaching in Greek though the nicknames he gave to his disciples were in the

Aramaic of his Northern Galilee dialect. But if Jesus is to be well understood by Judeans he would have needed to use Greek or the more ancient classical Hebrew because his northern dialect would be misunderstood as much as understood. This is the reason Saint Luke transliterates our Lord's cry on the cross "My God, my God why hast thou forsaken me?" Matthew and Luke narrate these words in the Aramaic tongue of Jesus' Northern dialect. Jesus near the end of his suffering on the cross speaks the language of his childhood when he cries out the great Psalm 22 and as the gospel writers tell us those who heard him at the cross misunderstood what he said (Mt 27:45-50).

The word *joy* is a powerful word and it is a word highly charged with feelings, as each use of the word in the New Testament demonstrates.

Of all modern writers I think it is C.S. Lewis who best understood the word. It was a very important word for him and he actually titled his autobiography of the early years of his Christian journey with the fascinating title *Surprised by Joy*. Lewis was a superb philologist and he realized the play of words in his title. Its real meaning therefore is "Surprised by Surprise." He describes *joy* in his chapter on laughter in *The Screwtape Letters*:

> You will see [joy] among friends and lovers reunited on the eve of a holiday. Among adults some pretext in the way of Jokes is usually provided, but the facility with which the smallest witticisms produce laughter at such a time shows that they are not the real cause. What the real cause is we do not know. Something like it is expressed in much of that detestable art which humans call Music, and something like it occurs in Heaven—a meaningless acceleration in the rythm of celestial experience, quite opaque to us.

I think Lewis has it perfectly! Joy is *meaningful*. (Remember that the book is written from the perspective of a demon who is renouncing great truth.) Joy is not the hollow laughter of disorientation because there are wondrous but understandable reasons for joy. James knew the healthiness that results from the discovery that trusting God produces real endurance in the real world. Our Lord portrays a sorrow that turns to joy because of the victory of his life over death. Paul sees the joy that comes from knowing Jesus as friend and companion and knowing that he is the one is near by. That reality is the good reason for joy.

Joy is rhythmic too. Joy is not hysterical. There can be the breakthrough of sheer exuberance and of robust excitement but in another equally joyous moment joy is the peaceful quietness of just feeling safe. Like the peace St. Paul describes to the Philippians because the "Lord is nearby."

Joy is at its core a relationship word that comes from the greatest of all relationships, the friendship that is ours with Jesus Christ. Joy is baffling to evil and always has been. Nothing is so troubling to the devil as the laughter of joy. It is an insult to the terror and gravity of hell. When Frodo and his loyal friend Sam Gamgee laugh out loud on the dark tower in J. R. R. Tolkien's *Lord of the Rings*, their laughter causes an earthquake because laughter was never heard at that place under Sauron's control. The two adventurers had challenged the evil of the ring and their present situation was perilous. But for a few moments they remember the shire which causes their laughter with its innocence as they thought of the stories of their homeland. That laughter was a prelude to the collapse of the power of Sauron. It reminds us of the fourth commandment: "You shall remember . . ." There is a profound power in remembering the goodness and faithfulness of God.

It is the mystery of joy's incredible power that Jesus shares with his disciples on the Thursday night of Holy Week. His promise is the prelude to the collapse of the power of sin, the power of death and the power of the evil one, the devil. Evil can not endure joy, because evil is focused inward and also because evil does not have a sense of humor.

Chapter Five

The Humor of the Unexpected

The humor of the unexpected discovery of incongruity is the most common cause of laughter. Little children hide behind a door and say "boo"; we laugh because they thought we thought they were someone else and they surprised us and sometimes they really do. There are many instances of the humorously unexpected surprise in New Testament accounts and they were the sources of laughter then as now. We either laugh or catch our breath when we expect to find one thing and something different happens that we were not expecting; if the unexpected is frightening and dangerous we shudder; if it is a welcome surprise we laugh. Our Lord's first miracle at Cana during a wedding celebration is an unexpected surprise in the second way. According to John's Gospel narrative (Jn 2), the mother of Jesus confronts her son at the wedding feast of a young couple; her intention is probably to remind Jesus that he and his disciples were socially obligated as guests to bring some gift to the wedding feast. She tells Jesus "They have no wine." What follows in the miracle at Cana is genuinely funny especially when the head waiter scolds the bridegroom for holding back the best wine. At that point the servants who had filled the jars with water as Jesus had told them probably whispered the incredible truth to the head waiter. John in his Gospel tells his readers that when this sign happened it showed the glory of Jesus and his disciples believed in him. Jesus gave this sign of transformation at the beginning of his ministry and it is a sign unexpected by everyone. What he did is celebrative and fun; it is humorous and yet wonderfully understated too in that Jesus does not announce to the guests and the couple, "Watch everyone, I will now do a miracle" but rather the servants who followed his strange instruction are the ones who gave it away to the head waiter, and the waiter in his complaint gives it away to the young married couple; the disciples find out too, and through them we know about the strange and wonderful wedding party at Cana.

Jesus the teacher also makes use of parables that are humorous through an unexpected turn in the story so that the humorous surprise takes up a major part in the story line of the parables.

The parable of the all day workers tells a story of those who earned the agreed upon wage for their all day work. But the surprise in the parable is that the eleventh hour workers received the same full day pay because of the generosity of the employer. There is a bittersweet humor in this parable: The laughter belongs to the one hour workers who could not imagine such a windfall of good fortune after they had spent most of a day worried about how they could earn enough money to feed their families and then by surprise near the end of the day they are employed and paid as if they had had a job all day. The all day workers complained but that is human nature and we who know ourselves expected this complaint. Nevertheless nothing takes away from the wonderful and improbable humor of an employer either so rich or so generous that he paid everyone the same. It was not necessary and yet he did it because he wanted to. The whole scene, complaints and all, is very funny because we could not have expected something so good, so contrary to ordinary experience, to happen right in front of our eyes.

One evening a distinguished Pharisee named Nicodemus comes to Jesus to talk about Kingdom expectations. In the middle of their conversation Jesus makes an unexpected statement to this man of stature and learning. "Unless you are born again you can not see the Kingdom of God." Nicodemus sees the humor in Jesus' statement and proves it by his reply, "How can I? Do I enter my mother's womb again . . ." (Jn 3). This is the encounter of two strong people and its humorous beginning dialogue results in the clear teaching of Jesus about the new birth that comes from above by the saving act of God.

On the road to Emmaus following the resurrection of Jesus a scene of shocked expectation and humorous surprise is Luke's most important Easter narrative. Two travelers enroute to Emmaus meet up with another traveler who they do not recognize and the two invite their new acquaintance to stay with them for a meal. He seems unaware of their grief as they lament the death of Jesus. "Are you the only one who does not know of the tragedy of the death of our friend, Jesus?" Their traveling companion then tells them beginning with the witness of Old Testament scripture of the meaning of the death of Jesus in their behalf and at one amazing moment in their meal together Jesus, who was the one they did not recognize, vanishes from their presence. They could only say "How our hearts were warmed when he spoke to us!" This road to Emmaus event is humorous in the grand tradition of the unexpected surprise. Why should the risen Lord find two ordinary disciples, not even among the original twelve and why would he walk with them? Why would he listen to these two as they told of their grief as if he did not know the story already? The whole experience is wonderfully joyous and has about it the excitement of a great humorous moment. It is the humor of not knowing how great and famous is the person you are near and then in a surprise breakthrough the discovery happens. There is the story of a child who broke away from his parents on the front row of a concert hall when they had come to attend a piano recital, the child went to the piano on the concert stage while the audience was filing in for a piano performance by the great Paderewski that was to later take place in that great hall. Before his parents knew where he was they saw to their considerable embarrassment that their child was on the great stage and he had climbed upon the piano bench. The little boy was playing his childhood lesson of "twinkle, twinkle little star" as his horrified mother and father were trying to get to the stage and retrieve their youngster. At that moment, the great pianist, Paderewski, hushed the parents and quietly came up to the piano behind the lad and whispered to him to keep playing his song. Then the master musician placed his large hands alongside of the lad's and played a beautiful and gentle ornamentation to the tune of the boy. Together they had played Mozart's magnificent song and the audience roared its approval. The small child only knew of a nice man who helped his song along, but the audience knew more and in that unexpected surprise were the ingredients of a profound kind of humor. We are grateful that St. Luke has narrated for us that same sort of revelation moment that happened to two disciples on the road to Emmaus.

The humor of the unexpected does have the element of fright as a part of the dynamics of laughter. When a scary shock turns out to be good, it then becomes funny. This is a key feature in children's games and stories. There is bad shock that comes from the fright because of evil and danger; this shock causes a clearing of the head and the sudden rush of adrenaline so that a human being is able to act in a response of flight or fight, but good fright is the shock prelude to the most expansive laughter of the whole self. The role that the experience of fright played is to draw together the whole self and to clear the head, stir up the adrenaline in a way that makes the laughter when it comes whole and complete. The greatest adventure stories succeed best if they are able to contain both kinds of fright. On any list of the twelve greatest films ever made is *The Wizard of Oz* because everything about the film is superb as a story of adventure, of self discovery, of friendship, of the angst of fear, and of resolution. The film really works in all these themes because there are the two kinds of fright as fundamental ingredients in the story, and the two play off of each other. There is a small girl who falls into a pig-pen at the beginning of the story and a terrified farm worker, as frightened as he is, still manages to rescue the girl whose name is Dorothy. Afterward the farm hand faints because he is sure that he is a coward at heart, yet he had exposed himself to danger and he had rescued a little careless girl. Later in Dorothy's dream she and her three companions meet the terror of the Witch of the East who is dreadful and powerful as she has surrounded herself with an army of flying demon-like monsters. As evil as she is, there is one flaw in her apparent invincibility but the four companions who are caught in her castle only discover this weakness of the witch when they are attempting to save their friend, the Scarecrow from burning after the witch threw a flash of fire upon him. They throw water on the Scarecrow and it splashes on the witch. This is her fatal weakness in that she cannot touch water, and it destroys her. Many children have had bad dreams about the scenes in the witch's tower with her flying demon-like servants, it is because the fright she created was cruel and its goal was to capture Dorothy in order to gain possession of the magic shoes that Dorothy was wearing. It is the fright of terror in the face of apparently unlimited power to harm.

But children do not have nightmare dreams about the smoke-filled great hallway of the mighty Oz which at first seems so awesome; why is this so? It is because the frightening experience of the four friends before Oz is a prelude to a surprising resolution. The little dog Toto pulls at a curtain and reveals Oz as the Kansas carnival man who Dorothy had met before when she was trying to run away with Toto. But the old magician is a wise man and he confers gifts to Dorothy's friends that causes every audience to laugh and sometimes cry because like all really well told adventure stories the humor of the award scene in *Wizard of Oz* is profound as it connects with who we are and what we feel about ourselves. The story dared to face up to primary human fears concerning courage, intelligence, the ability to love and the most fundamental childhood fear of all, finding the way home. The story frightened us at every level and then in the end the fright turns to sheer fun and resolution. What made it work was that the final fright prepared us to be wide awake for the laughter of joy at the end of the story.

This very kind of fright as a prelude to laughter, plays a major role in the deep gladness of the New Testament's basic story and centerpoint. The shock of the unexpected is the center point of the whole story of good news.

C.S. Lewis became a believer in Jesus Christ when he was a young don at Oxford University. He had become an atheist when he was 17 years of age, then finally he grudgingly believed in the existence of God in his mid-twenties but he still could not understand or fit into the whole picture, the central importance of Jesus Christ that Christianity claims. One evening the young scholar, Lewis and two friends from Oxford, Edward Dyson and J.R.R. Tolkien were debating this central issue. Tolkien made this argument with Lewis. He reminded Lewis of their common love for adventure stories which was then and would continue to be a key linkage in their friendship. In adventures there must be two elements, he argued, the sense of catastrophe and the sense of eucatastrophe. (The prefix *eu* in the Greek language means "good") Tolkien then made a telling and convincing point to his friend, Lewis. The good catastrophe in the greatest adventure stories is greater than the catastrophe in those stories. We have in all adventure stories imagined, the terror of catastrophe and then imagined, the exciting resolution that comes from the good catastrophe. Tolkien then dared to make his boldest statement. "Jesus Christ is the eucatastrophe of all time— except that he is true." The next day Lewis wrote in a letter to his friend, Arthur Greeves, "I rode in my brother's motorcycle side car to Whipsnade Zoo today. At the beginning of the ride I did not believe in Jesus Christ, at the end of the ride I did. Nothing particular happened on the ride but the long talk last night with Dyson and Tolkien had much to do with it."

G. K. Chesterton calls this good news "the enormous exception ... news that seems too good to be true ... that God has visited this planet in person." This is the fright that the night shift shepherds experienced when Jesus was born. There should always be visitors who come when a baby is born to make sure things are okay with a family at the time of birth, but not just anyone should come. God in his wisdom decides Joseph and Mary should have visitors too. They have the total surprise of the wealthy foreign magi who bring very valuable gifts: gold and two fragrances. But the best visit comes from a handful of sheepherders who had night shift duty and it all began for them with an unexpected fright! The angel appears to them "and they were sore afraid." "Terrified" is the word used here to explain their fright. But the fear is turned into joy as the angel of the Lord is joined with a great choir to sing for these shepherds the first Christmas carol. This whole event is funny and worshipful at the same moment. They were invited to visit the Holy family as were the wise men—but not Herod. God makes his own choices.

Chapter Six

The Humor of Repetition

The humor of repetition, like the humor of the unexpected, is a very succinct and uncomplicated ingredient in comedy. Something becomes funny because it is repeated and in the repetition we find ourselves laughing at that something that is often very ordinary, but as it is repeated it becomes comical.

Hebrew poetry depends upon restatement as the most recognizable feature in its literary form. This restatement literary device is called parallelism. Throughout the Psalms and the Prophets we expect every writer to say a theme one way and then to say it again in a slightly different way. This use of repetition becomes a powerful and communicative clarifier for Jewish poetry. The writer of Ecclesiastes wants to make the point that the more knowledge we have then the greater is our distress and he writes this theme twice to really make his point: "For in much wisdom is much vexation, and he who increases knowledge increases sorrow"(Eccl 1:18).

The repetition of Hebrew parallelism also makes use of parallel contrasts in the same way as parallel similarity. Listen to the same writer make a powerful use of contrasting parallelism:

"The heart of the wise is in the house of mourning; but the heart of fools is in the house of mirth"(Eccl 7:4). The two sentences are parallel and identical except for four words that create a parallel contrast. Within this repetitious pattern we find most of the humor of the Old Testament writers. Notice now the example of a humorous reflection by the preacher of Ecclesiastes on those people who can never decide what or when to do what needs to be done because they are always waiting for a perfect time to act: "He who observes the wind will not sow and he who regards the clouds will not reap"(Eccl 11:4). There is something funny about people who can never decide what to do and yet persist in consulting their advisors continually. "My therapist thinks that right now I should be more assertive about showing affection. My therapist also thinks I should not let anyone get too close to me right now."

The use of repetition also makes it possible to increase the intensity and the humor level at each telling. This enables the repetition to build toward either a surprise fulfillment or a surprise let down. The cynical preacher of Ecclesiastes makes use of this kind of repetition, too. "Bread is made for laughter, and wine gladdens life, and money answers everything" (Eccl 10:19). Since tradition has it that the writer is the fabulously wealthy Solomon we know that this repetitious build up is leading the reader to a humorous let down. Solomon, prepared us for this let down when earlier on he made it clear as a rich man that money did not buy happiness: "He who loves money will not be satisfied with money . . ." (Eccl 5:10).

Repetition may also lead toward a fulfillment too. Solomon, in spite of his cynicism about what he calls the vapor of life (the word in our English text is translated "vanity", but it is not the Hebrew word "empty" but the word "vapor." This difference is a major difference, too. Solomon develops a repetitious poem in Ecclesiastes that becomes the high point of the book:

> For everything there is a season, and a time for every mat-
> ter under heaven: a time to be born, and a time to die; a
> time to plant, and a time to pluck up what is planted; a time
> to kill, and a time to heal; a time to break down, and a time
> to build up; a time to weep, and a time to laugh; a time to

mourn, and a time to dance; a time to case away stones, and a time to gather stones together; a time to embrace, and a time to refrain from embracing; a time to seek, and a time to lose; a time to keep, and a time to cast away; a time to rend, and a time to sew; a time to keep silence, and a time to speak; a time to love, and a time to hate; a time for war, and a time for peace.

(Ecclesiastes 3:1-8)

This poem has moved beyond the territory of a bitter and disillusioned king's thoughts about the vapor of his life. The poem stirs us up to want to find the only one who can make sense of these seasons of our lives. The words of mirth like embrace, are united with the stormy words we do not want to hear. We see in this repetitious poem the two masks that become the symbols of Greek drama, both tragedy and comedy but this poem was written almost 500 years earlier than the Greeks thought of the same theme.

When Jesus tells parables he is a master at the use of repetitious humor and pathos. Luke narrates three parables that Jesus told in dramatic sequence. (Luke 15): Jesus first tells of 99 sheep safe at their rockery and one that is lost in the wild. By surprise the shepherd leaves the 99 and finds the one. This is followed with celebration. Then Jesus tells of a woman with ten coins but who realizes that one coin is missing. She also follows her hard work and success in finding the one stray coin with a party. The third story is of a man with two sons. These three parables show a whimsical and exciting use of repetitious humor. Each story is the same; each story builds in intensity, and each story is humorous at different levels. From these parables we make a major theological discovery, too, we discover that in Heaven itself there is laughter when one sinner repents. We never expected such a resounding answer to the pessimism of Solomon in his Ecclesiastes. We never expected that our lives mattered that much to God. If we are vapor, we are vapors that matters!

Our Lord makes use of the humor of repetition in a wonderfully healing way in the life of the disciple Peter. Luke tells us that it was at a fishing incident on the Lake of Tiberius where Jesus first won Peter as his disciple (Luke 5). In John's gospel we learn from John that following the victory of Jesus on Easter the one disciple who is still at a loss with his own inner discouragement and loss of confidence is Peter. John is the gospel writer who helps us really understand his friend Peter and how he was restored to apostolic early church leadership from the shadows of regret at having denied his Lord. John records for us that Peter decided to leave Judea and return to Galilee following the amazing events of Holy Week. "I'm going fishing." His friends decide to go with him which is a very good thing for friends to do when they know how discouraged Peter is in his heart. They fish all night, which is the custom for Lake of Galilee fishermen, but they catch nothing. Jesus finds them and calls to them from the shore, "Have you caught anything, lads?" They answer, "No." He then calls out; "Put your nets on the other side and you will catch some." When they do they bring in a haul of fish and John shouts out to his companions, "It's the Lord." With that Peter jumps into the water and comes ashore. Jesus had first won Peter as his disciple when he outfished him on Galilee and now in the time of Peter's discouragement Jesus assures his friend with another catch of fish and a breakfast fire at dawn. The whole scene is humorous as well as encouraging.

The three repetitious questions of Jesus to Peter that follows this lakeside breakfast are another example of the use of repetition that has about it a troubling aspect for Peter but at its core there is the unmistakable mark of humor too. The sense of the three questions are: "Peter, do you love me more than these fish?" And three times Jesus clearly reaffirms Peter's leadership with the challenge to carry on his mandate: "Feed my sheep." There is also the threefold resolution for Peter of three denials that had caused him to weep bitterly on the terrible Friday of his cowardness and defeat. Jesus now brings Peter through the regret of three denials by means of three good questions, "Do you love me, Peter?" He had also brought full circle this man who was from the beginning a Galilean fisherman and fulfilled the first prophecy that Jesus had made concerning Peter, "I will make you a fisher of men"(Lk 5). The humor of repetition made the connection clear and understandable. It also becomes a heart warming and encouraging narrative for us who later read it as well. We need to know that human defeat because of weakness and fear is not the last word. It only may be the next to the last word, but Jesus himself has the last word. We need to know this. We also need to know that Jesus is able to find us when we are discouraged and think that we want to be alone, or that we need to be alone, or that we are condemned to be alone. Jesus answers all the questions with the humor of the events at the lakeside and he does it with very few words.

Chapter Seven
The Humor of Justice

There is a humor with justice as its motive energy. The humor of justice has saltiness about it because it is the laughter that accompanies the vindication of truth as it wins out over falsehood. What enriches the laughter of justice in the New Testament is the fact that the very word for justice in the Greek language, *dikiaos,* is the word that is translated, depending on its context, by three English words: *justice, righteousness,* or *justification.* Since God is the only judge and since he is the one able to heal and make right what is broken, the good news of Christ is highly focused around this very word. Human sin is defined in relationship to the righteousness of God as the standard which human sins offend against and defy. But when God's righteousness in Jesus Christ acts toward us and in our behalf, the result is a victory over the power of sin over the finality of death and over the power of the tempter, the Devil. The result is justification, which means that the righteousness of Jesus Christ is granted by God in our behalf and toward our healing and restoration. Usually this salvation happens by surprise. We do not expect such a breakthrough of rightness in our favor by the one who is judge of all the earth. It is this very good news surprise that St. Paul places at the heart of his song at the close of Romans 8. "If God is for us who can be against us? Who is to condemn us?" (Paul uses a harsh and final word here; the word *katakrino* which means to speak down or judge down upon a condemned person, to say the final terrible word against a man or woman that only a judge can do) then St. Paul answers his question, "Is it Christ Jesus? Yes." We now learn that indeed Jesus Christ alone has the right to the last word; to speak as the one who has the holy right to condemn because he is the just one. But Paul then announces his surprise to the Romans that receive his letter. "Yes, this very Jesus Christ is the one who died and who lives and indeed intercedes for us . . . Who can separate us from the love of Christ? . . . I am convinced that neither height or depth . . ." (Rom 8). Here in this song of Paul's letter to the Romans we see both the righteousness of Christ and the justification of man/woman brought together in what can only be called the gospel, the good news of salvation by surprise.

The triumph of truth over falsehood is a serious and solemn matter because so much is at stake. There is nothing funny about injustice when it happens to and against people. We recoil when the cruelty and destructiveness of men and women is revealed in a criminal court room because we can see before us the real harm that has happened to the lives of real people in real places. We demand justice and we expect it. We will not feel safe nor in fact are we safe in a jungle or a city where injustice and raw blatant use of power is unchallenged or unjudged. Finally, sooner or later, there must be an accounting, a leveling of the mountains and valleys (Isa 40). If there is not this leveling and righteous weighing of justice then the created order is amoral and if that is the true state of affairs then our only hope is to make friends with those who have the most raw power. It will mean that all of our jokes and all humor will be the humor of cynicism, like the humor in a harsh Berlin cafe as captured in the musical *Cabaret*, where those who now appear strong, taunt and mock those who now appear weak. When might makes right then it would be true that "life is a cabaret." All humor would at last reduce to the jokes against the weak and those who are hated. Comedy in the cabaret is the comedy of chaos where despair and power would be watched by comedians for their funny quirks. As those who are the targets of derision are the object of laughter.

The Bible holds two themes together and these two themes make all the difference. The first is that the human story even if we are not aware of it is boundried by God's righteousness. The story we call life is not amoral or immoral but it is by God's decision moral and subject to profound consequences. This is the justice of God that surrounds the whole human story. The second theme is that within the boundary of that story God has provided by his decision for real freedom by the human characters in that story.

The first freedom word that appears in the Bible is the word *dominion*. It was given by God to the man and woman (Gen 1). We have a degree and quality of authority and freedom that the rest of creation does not enjoy. *We* name the animals. Every other part of the reality that accompanies us on our journey through this story gets its name from man/woman. We are the stewards of creation. The word translated "dominion" from ancient Hebrew means literally "to tread" as a worker treads grapes. God makes the grapes, we make the wine, and God holds us accountable for what we do with both the grapes and the wine. Our bad choices have consequences that harm our stewardship of life, and our wise choices have consequences that help our stewardship of life. The history time/event line of our human story is turbulent because of the freedom God has granted man and woman. There are the strong downward strokes of our bad choices that do real harm within our story. There are also the positive strokes when the restraint of terror has happened and when positive good happens within our story. We have an uneven but fascinating history that describes our life and our stewardship of the earth. I remember when I was an undergraduate freshman at the University of California in Berkeley, California in 1949. The common joke in those days in Berkeley was of the smell of the Berkeley estuary. This part of San Francisco Bay was so badly contaminated that there were almost no fish in the estuary and for those hearty athletes who rowed for the Cal crew there was the smell of contaminated water that greeted them every morning. I returned to Berkeley in 1970 when I became the pastor of the First Presbyterian Church of Berkeley. When our family moved to Berkeley in 1970 everything had changed in my old college town and one positive change was that the bay had been restored by wise stewardship decisions of the communities of the bay. Fish had returned to such an extent that the Berkeley pier had become the number one recreational site of the entire Bay area. One songwriter would even write a hit song about the marvelous sea breezes and the fishing possibilities in that pier—"Sittin' by the Dock in the Bay." It would have been a different song in 1949!

The eternal decision of God is the boundary that surrounds our human story. "In the beginning was the Word" (Jn 1). God spoke and by that speech creation happened. God's speech is also the fulfillment of the story. But there is more. God spoke into the story too. "The word became flesh and dwelt among us full of grace and truth" (Jn 1). Jesus Christ is God speaking for himself and through him everything that exists came into being. He stands at history's close as its fulfillment; He stands at its beginning. "All things were made through him," and he stands at history's center as the Redeemer who is able to make sense of the whole story. Jesus Christ as Redeemer does not destroy the freedom of the men and women who are also in the story; he enters our story in our behalf and this is the good news event that the Old Testament points toward in hopeful anticipation and the New Testament points to in grateful witness.

Jesus the judge, the righteous one, the author of justification makes use of the humor of justice to clear the air and to encourage us to see into ourselves and our motives and to look closely at our freedoms and at our captivities. The indirectness that is a feature in all humor enables us to see ourselves more clearly than would be possible if we were directly confronted with even a small part of the whole truth about ourselves. During the feast of Tabernacles Jesus is in Jerusalem and John's gospel tells its readers of a confrontation with Jesus that happens in which a woman caught in the act of adultery is brought before Jesus. He is told by those who have brought the woman that the Levitical code requires that she be stoned. (Actually the Levitical text says that the man and woman caught in adultery were to be stoned by the community while making use of the safeguards of trial with witnesses so that with safeguards the community rules upon their guilt before punishment is executed.) The crowd asks Jesus, "What do you say about her?" It is the expectation of first century tradition that a Rabbi is asked for his commentary upon the law. It is also expected that a teacher of the law would also be a wise judge of guilt. The cynical part of this incident rests in the present tense reality of the Jewish culture at the time of the event. A Roman decree throughout its empire prohibited any action by local populations that would result in riots. Therefore any decision by the Jewish Sanhedrin that would require lethal judgment could only be executed by the approved Roman tribunal. The right of the sword belonged only to Rome itself. The one exception in the Palestine of the first century was that Herod as king was allowed the power of capital punishment. Were Jesus to authorize the stoning of this accused woman he would be guilty of inciting to riot under Roman law. However, if Jesus speaks in favor of the accused woman then he has weakened for some of the people his claim as a fearless teacher and upholder of the law. John who writes this narrative calls the question of the crowd a temptation of Jesus.[1]

What Jesus does and what he says in this highly inflamed and dangerous moment are both wise and humorous responses to a dangerous moment. First he slows everything down by stooping over and by writing in the sandy soil. Every comedian knows that timing is an essential ingredient to all humor. The best and most experienced humorists are the ones who take their time slowing everything down to prepare an audience for the fulfillment line of a story. Garrison Keillor, like Mark Twain, possesses that ability to insist that an audience wait patiently to hear him out in the telling of a story about Lake Woebegone. Mark Twain forces his reader in one of his stories about the proud California blue jay to wait for three pages for one very funny sentence at the very end of his elaborate blue jay yarn. In the Mark Twain tale an owl from Canada stopped by to see what had so agitated the blue jays in this Sierra farm with its deserted barn. The blue jays had become hysterical in their laughter at one hapless blue jay

1. There are N. T. interpreters who have challenged the placement of this incident here in John 8:1-4 and the narrative is suppressed in several ancient Eastern manuscripts possibly because some scribal sponsors may have concluded that the text did not stand clearly against the sin of adultery. It is my conviction that the text belongs exactly in this place where the western manuscripts have placed it. It is authentic and necessary to the whole text. See the argument in my commentary on the gospel of John, *The Book That John Wrote* (Vancouver: Regent College Publishing, 2000).

who filled a barn with acorns. Mark Twain tells us that the owl from Canada was not that impressed by the commotion. "But then he wasn't that impressed by Yosemite either." This is one of Mark Twain's funniest lines and we must read four pages to find it. But that is part of the humor in the story. We had been led to expect more from this owl, and an owl from Canada at that. We cannot even imagine someone not impressed by Yosemite and that is funny too. But it took the waiting to experience the humor. Jesus has very much at stake when he slows down an angry, insistent and demanding crowd so that they will really hear a single sentence he has for them; he dares to slow everything down to silence. At the right moment he spoke: "He said to them 'He who is without sin let him be the first to throw a stone at her' and then he stooped down and continued to write in the sand" (Jn 8). John tells us that from the oldest to the youngest they all left and went away. This is righteous humor because it connects the listener to his or her own obedience to the law of God. It makes the connection in an indirect way but the connection is inescapable and the result is that Jesus protects the woman who has been accused and he has also protected the crowd from doing more harm to their souls than they already have. Already they have tempted the Lord and they were at the edge of committing murder. Jesus has spared them from that terrible act. The role of his humorous act is heightened by his writing in the sand words or pictures that no one can as far as we can tell in the crowd is able to read and then the impossible sentence that no one can escape. Jesus has given to us an unforgettable example of the humor of justice. Best of all the humor of justice is humor in our behalf.

Chapter Eight

The Humor of Misunderstanding

Misunderstandings and misinformation are the common source of the worst kinds of tragedy, as in the confusion of a sea captain or jet pilot who has been making navigational decisions on the basis of data that he or she did not understand or understood in an incorrect way. But if the misunderstanding does not have such grave consequences then such misunderstandings become the source of laughter. In an earlier chapter I recalled how Big Bird from Sesame Street is excited to sing about the longest word he has ever seen: "ABCDEFGHIJKLMNOPQRSTUVWXYZ." His friends help Big Bird realize he has seen the alphabet, not a word. This form of humor has the good effect of reminding us to listen closely to what is said and to notice that things are not always what we first thought they were. Our first impressions need to be closely examined. Words are collections of letters, but not all collections of letters are meant to be words.

Jesus understands the communication and teaching importance of this kind of humor, and he makes skillful use of the humor of misunderstanding as a way to enlarge understanding.

One example of this is in the parable of the mustard seed (Mt 13). The tiny mustard seed seems too insignificant to matter in the large scale of things and when we first see it we are in danger of writing off its importance. We see a seed so small it is more like a dust particle than a real seed. But we misunderstand what we have seen because that seed will become a bush of such strength that birds make their nests in its branches. We laugh at ourselves for having made such a mistake. We trusted a first impression that was botanically in error rather than well informed. Jesus uses this humorous parable to teach about the powerful and growing nature of his kingly reign. The life of an ordinary person seems insignificant at first glance and such a small factor point when weighed alongside the more apparently awesome forces of history, but Jesus has now opened up a new possibility by his humorous attack upon our first impression about what constitutes future significance. We now know that even one small beginning point such as one person who trusts in God is like that mustard seed or the hidden invisible leaven in a heap of moist flour. One of the comedy songs in the musical *Les Miserables* makes the same point as a young street urchin sings a song about little people and he warns those who now seem so powerful that they should watch out because the "pup grows up." The mustard seed stays small only at the beginning. There is no stopping it when it starts to grow.

Jesus makes use of this human tendency toward misunderstanding as a major teaching theme not only in parables, but also in his didactive teaching. Jesus begins the Sermon on the Mount, which is his commentary on the law, in the same way as the great song of the Torah begins. Psalm 1 tells of the blessedness of the way of righteousness. "Blessed is the man or woman who walks in the law of the Lord . . ." The Hebrew word for "blessed" here is *ashre*. This word means to find the right road, therefore roadway language dominates the Torah psalms. In both Psalm 1 and Psalm 119 those who are faithful to God "walk in the way of the law." Jesus begins his sermon in Matthew 5 in the same way. He also uses the word "blessed" and in the same roadway sense as Psalm 1. This passage offers a useful example to readers of the New Testament that though the Greek language is used, the thoughts underneath the Greek words are Hebrew meanings.

Jesus is saying in his nine blessings at the opening of the Sermon on the Mount, "You are on the right road when you are poor in Spirit." But now humorous surprises confront those who hear this sermon. Jesus surprises every ordinary expectation with a surprise that humorously challenges what we would ordinarily think. Who would think that there is anything good about being poor in spirit or poor in any way?

How could poverty be the right road? But Jesus has a surprise for us. He tells us that our first impression is a misunderstanding of the true nature of reality. We are on the right road when we face up to our poverty in spirit, when we face our need for the nourishment of our spirits provided there is the one who is rich enough to answer that need. Mourning is also the right road if there is one who comforts nearby. The beatitudes show that at first glance we misunderstand the reality of the covenant promises of God. Because of God's promise the expectations that we originally thought we were certain of are now swept up into a radically new order which Jesus calls the fulfillment of the law (Mt 5): "Think not that I have come to destroy the law . . . I have come to fulfill the law." The word "blessed" which as a Greek word means "happy," but in its Hebrew sense means "walking in the way" is the word Jesus chose to signal this new road.

St. Paul was able to make sense of his physical handicap through this same humor that Jesus puts at the beginning of the Sermon on the Mount. It is almost certain that Paul had some form of eye disease. One clue to this is his non-recognition of the high priest while he is on trial in Jerusalem. He spoke boldly to the high priest and people near by struck Paul for his lack of respect for the high priest. Paul answers, "I'm sorry I did not know it was the high priest" (Acts 23). He also writes to the Galatians, "You would have gladly plucked your eyes out for me." This is another reference to his eye problem. He also says to them in his final written greeting, "See what large letters I write this to you" (Gal 6). We also are told in 1 Corinthians that the people say of Paul, "He writes weighty letters but when you see him you will not be impressed" (2 Cor 10). These references offer clues that cause interpreters to wonder if Paul's "thorn in the flesh" was his bad eyesight or even possibly cataracts which gave a clouded look to his eyes. In the church at Corinth Paul is accused by one of the leaders in that church who is a faith healer that Paul's physical health crisis is a sign of a larger spiritual flaw in his character. Paul decides that he must answer that personal charge against him in order to sustain his pastoral usefulness to the Christians at Corinth. We, who years later read his letters to the Corinthians, are grateful that Paul decided to answer the new teachers at Corinth because of the way he offers a highly personal commentary on the blessings of Jesus from the Sermon on the Mount. They wonder why he has not experienced the gift of healing. Paul tells his friends at Corinth that three times he did pray to God for a victory over his thorn in the flesh but three times the answer came back to him. "My grace is sufficient for you." It is then that Paul tells us all through his words to a confused church at Corinth, "When I am weak then I am strong" (2 Cor 12). We need to hear that humorous word from Paul because we have always thought it was strength that produces more strength. We thought that if we are strong that would certainly be the sign of spiritual maturity and that the ability to conquer illnesses would be the best sign and wonder of all! But Paul heard Jesus' answer to his prayer and better yet he knows the Jesus who hears his prayers. Paul clears the air for us concerning one of our most common misunderstandings. The best part is that Paul focuses our eyes on the love of God as the greatest strength and the greatest sign, just as he did in 1 Corinthians 13, "My grace is sufficient."

Chapter Nine
The Humor of Exaggeration

E xaggeration can be very funny. It is also one more way that humor is able to help me see in bold relief both the distinctive positive marks as well as the quirks of my personality. By exaggeration the unique and sometimes troublesome traits of my personality are outlined more understandably than would be the case if someone who knows them or suffers them would be able to explain them to me in direct or prosaic language. It is the special role of the circus clowns and the court jesters in the history of comedy who play this special role. I think the funniest humorist clown in American comedy is Jonathan Winters and no one has matched his ability at the outlandish humor of exaggeration. Winters has a one-man comedy sketch about airplanes and the fear that people have concerning air flight. His sketch faces up to our questions about the service and safety of flying as well as the competency of the companies that dare to transport paying human customers high above the ground. Winters includes every worry and exaggerates them all with his sketch about the world's oldest flight attendant and airline president. Winters plays her in his sketch. She is

Maude Rickert who not only owns the company but flies along as a flight attendant with the *Maude Rickert Airline and Screen Door Company*. They fly DC-1s. Winters is funny because he presses each theme beyond the boundary where ordinary logic would allow. It is through this exaggeration that the comedian enables an emotional connection to happen so that we are permitted to see how ordinary elements in our own character or behavior look if they are magnified by the art of the humorist's exaggeration.

The exaggeration or hyperbole of the Bible is deeply rooted in Hebrew poetry and was well understood in the time of the first century. The song-writers of the Old Testament were masterful in the use of exaggeration as an essential element in the poetry of the Bible.

Jeremiah complains to the Lord about the difficulty of his mandate to be a prophet of the Lord to kings and the people at Jerusalem who refuse to hear what the Lord's prophet is saying to them. What bothers Jeremiah even more is that as he observes the life of the people what he sees is that the wicked seem to prosper more than the righteous. These complaints about the dangers of the life of the lonely righteous prophet converge in upon Jeremiah and he prays to God about them. (Jer 12:1-5). "Righteous art thou, O Lord, when I complain to thee. . . . Why does the way of the wicked prosper?" Jeremiah then makes the request that God bring down severe judgment upon such people. He has concrete suggestions to make: "Pull them out like sheep for the slaughter and set them apart for the day of slaughter." But, as the book of Jeremiah will reveal to us, God has a profounder plan in mind than Jeremiah could imagine. In the meantime, the Lord decides to answer Jeremiah's prayer, and the answer is a shock to the complaining prophet. "If you have raced with men on foot, and they have wearied you, how will you compete with horses?" The answer of the Lord to his servant is both good news and bad news. First, "Jeremiah if you think this is bad, it is going to get worse." That is the bad news. The good news is that God is saying to his complaining young prophet, "Jeremiah, think of it! You will compete in a bigger race than you are now facing!" That is the good news because it makes clear that Jeremiah will be in the race and that can only happen if God makes it possible for him to be there. This reply to Jeremiah is humorous to us as we read it, even if not to him, and the humor lies in the exaggeration. No man can run against a horse and therefore we see immediately how funny is the Lord's answer to his servant, "You are having a hard time running against men, wait until tomorrow when I bring in the horses." But there is a promise hidden in the exaggerated answer and the story of Jeremiah makes the promise clear this brave prophet will indeed compete with horses and power greater than any horse. The importance of this text with its complaint by Jeremiah and the humor of the Lord is clear. We now better understand both Jeremiah and God. It is a disclosure text for us.

The poetry of exaggeration is found in the texts of hope and promise as well as in the texts of disclosure. Whereas the promise element in the Jeremiah encounter with God is hidden and only present by inference, there are places where the promise is crystal clear. In these instances the exaggeration presses upon us the full wonder of the promise. In Isaiah 40, the Lord speaks to the people through the prophet, "Why do you say, O Jacob, my way is hid from the Lord . . . Have you not known? . . . The Lord does not faint or grow weary . . . He gives power to the faint. . . ." We notice immediately that there is a remarkable similarity in the psychological ingredients between this text and the prayer of Jeremiah. Jeremiah is fatigued and weary and ready to faint and therefore he prays to the Lord as if the Lord is unaware of the dangers that he faces. In his case, he has an idea that he is sure will help him—the swift destruction of the people who are succeeding around him through the ways of evil while he flounders as he stays faithful to the ways of righteousness. The Lord's answer is to assure him that he will indeed continue to compete and against even greater opposition, which is exactly what happens as the readers of Jeremiah know.

The Lord also gives his people through the prophet Isaiah an answer to their worries about abandonment that is almost identical in essential content to the answer given by the Lord to Jeremiah. In the Isaiah text, like the Jeremiah text, the humor of exaggeration will also be an essential part of the Lord's word.

"The Lord does not faint or grow weary, his understanding is unsearchable. He gives power to the faint . . . even youths shall faint and be weary, and young men shall fall exhausted; but they who wait for the Lord shall renew their strength, they shall mount up with wings like eagles, they shall run and not be weary, they shall walk and not faint" (Isa 40). This is a beloved promise to those who feel the fatigue that comes when hope seems to vanish and loneliness sets in to take control. At the heart of the promise is a marvelous exaggeration, and one that is especially fun for a child who hears this promise. What boy or girl would not want to glide with the thermal winds like an eagle? But the exaggeration is still an exaggeration; people do not have wings as the promise tells us and everyone knows that fact. Whoever heard of a race against a horse? But both of these exaggerations have the positive effect of assuring an exhausted people that there is a source of strength that is beyond their present understanding and their present experience. That fact is not an exaggeration at all; it is the profound reality that underpins the humorous exaggeration about horses and eagles.

Jesus teaches and tells parables in this same rich tradition of the humor of exaggeration. He has the same goals as we have just observed in Jeremiah and Isaiah. Exaggeration enables a man or woman to see themselves more clearly than is possible if only the language of realism is used. It also helps a man or woman to see the realistic terror of a realistic crisis by portraying that crisis in terms that are more extremely stated than a strictly defined and technically realistic portrayal would permit. The humor of these exaggerated portrayals lies in the exaggeration itself.

On one occasion Jesus challenged a group of Pharisees who prided themselves on their ability to offer precise definitions of the legal details of Sabbath law observance. Jesus said to them, "You strain at gnats and you swallow camels." This is a very humorous statement that exaggerates the special talents of the Pharisees as lawyers of the law. It oversimplifies their talents of precision and at the same time helps a Pharisee see the blind side of their interpretive skill. They discover themselves in the position of condemning Jesus for the healing act of love toward a paralyzed man who is walking away with his cot. The man had "labored" on the Sabbath but only because of the love that heals.

Jesus uses the shock of recognition that comes from exaggeration to surprise his disciples with grace. On one afternoon Jesus tells his disciples, "How hard it is for a rich man to enter the kingdom of heaven. It is easier for a camel to go through the eye of a needle than for a rich man to enter the kingdom of God." The disciples are clearly shocked by the stark impossibility in this statement of their teacher, and they express this shock to Jesus, "Who then can be saved?" Jesus answers them with a statement that preserves both God's sovereignty and God's grace. "With man it is impossible but with God nothing is impossible." It is as if Jesus has taken us back to the horses that Jeremiah must run against. The race is an impossibility without the help of God just as our entrance into the kingdom of God is impossible without the act of God's grace.

Examples of humorous exaggeration includes our Lord's blunt statement to his friend Peter in that great turning-point moment when Jesus sets his face toward Jerusalem and tells his disciples that he must face death. Peter, the brave leader (who carries a small sword to prove it), rebukes Jesus and proudly announces, "No Lord it will never happen to you." Jesus answers Peter, "Get behind me Satan." This is hyperbole at its most extreme. Peter is not Satan, the fallen angel, just as Peter is not an unfallen angel. This is a humorous yet startling reply to Peter's heroic rebuke of his Lord. The disciples would be able to laugh about this shocking rejoinder of Jesus, but his word to Peter and the other disciples is clearly heard through the exaggeration. They must not, indeed they *cannot* finally stand in the way of the journey that Jesus knows is his and his alone.

In all of these instances Jesus used exaggeration concerning our lives, our fears, our sins, our hopes and his destiny as Savior. These exaggerations are a part of the way that Jesus connects us to the character of God about whom there is no exaggeration.

Chapter Ten

The Humor of Irony

Plato and Greek philosophers after him made effective use of the humor of irony in the teaching design of Greek philosophy, poems, and stories. This is because Plato had made the centerpoint of his philosophy his fascination with the difference between appearance and reality. The hero in Plato's *Parable of the Cave* is the one who understands the difference between what only appears real and that essence or inner reality that constitutes the real truth of what we see and experience. Ordinary people, according to Plato, are satisfied with shadows whereas the "philosopher king" knows the true essence behind what everyone else sees as a shadow, an appearance. This platonic premise led to the unfortunate dualism in Greek philosophy by which the spiritual man or woman is understood in a way that for Platonism downgraded the reality of the physical in favor of the exaltation of the spiritual. This led to an essential misunderstanding in Platonism that has had some devastating effects on all of Western philosophy and anthropology. It led to the spiritualization of life and enabled a person who was smart enough to avoid ethical responsibility for actual, concrete behavior because of his or her insight into the greater "spiritual" realms of reality. It has often led to an inevitable down-grading of the "particular and earthy part of who I am" in favor of the "mystical spiritual part of who I am."

The New Testament agrees fully with the Old Testament that personhood consists of the wholeness of man/woman as a complex person that in Biblical faith's doctrine of creation is endorsed and welcomed by God as real. I am one whole being created by God and within that wholeness the spiritual as well as the physical are each a part of my createdness by God's good design. My physical self is not an appearance of apparent reality but is the real me and in that complexity I am the one created in the image of God. This also means that I am not God and never will be; nor is there a spiritual part of me that is divine though somehow presently trapped within the prison of my physical self. It is the whole of me that is beloved by God. It is the whole of me that experiences the crises of sin and it is the whole of me that experiences redemption. Finally, it is the whole of me in the future resurrection of the body that faces eternal hope.

Gnosticism, a heresy that challenged the Christian gospel at the end of the first century is an example of neo-platonism attempting to capture the "idea" of Jesus Christ and thereby spiritually transform that idea into a phantom-like Christ symbol, who could then be comfortably harmonized within a gnostic framework. The early Christians opposed this platonic redefinition of Jesus Christ and we have the history of that controversy spread across the writings of parts of the New Testament in letters such as 1 and 2 Corinthians, Colossians, 1 John and also in writings of the early church fathers. Gnostic theology is powerfully answered in the earliest Christian creedal statements, The Apostles Creed and the Nicean Creed. Both of these creeds insist on the real Jesus, who unlike a phantom spiritualized Christ, was "born of the virgin Mary, suffered under Pontius Pilate." This real man, Jesus Christ, actually died; he did not appear to die; his death was definite and concretely real, as is our own death "dead, buried, descended into the place of death." His victory over death is also concretely real for "on the third day he arose." The early Christians wanted no confusion on this essential beginning place for faith. Jesus Christ is the real man and his actual connectedness to our humanity is not a platonic appearance, it is the very stuff of reality. John Updike, in his poem "Seven Stanzas at Easter," states this biblical insistence on the wholeness of reality when he writes in his poem in the language of the twentieth century "Let us not mock God with metaphor."

Plato's influence in Western thinking has persisted into modern theology so that a neo-gnostic fascination with spiritualization, with metaphor, has been a continuous challenge to the robust and wholistic understanding of reality that is evident throughout the biblical narratives, poems and prophecies.

The humor of irony depends on a contrast between what only appears and what really is. This ironic contrast is at the edge of the platonic "appearance/reality" contrast, but the contrast is also within Jewish humor and New Testament humor but it features both sides of the irony as real; In biblical ironic humor the contrast is not between the real and the apparently real. The Jewish and New Testament humorists are therefore less complicated than are their Greek philosophical humorists on this point. A Jewish/Christian humorist embraces the whole of a person as significant and real. Not only that, but the whole of the earth is understood as concretely real. This way of looking at life greatly multiplies the possibility for humor. It also opens up the possibility of God's judgment and God's love as events that a whole man or woman can experience in their whole self complete with hugs, and tears, and laughter. This concreteness is much more exciting than the non-concrete spiritualized intellectual insights of the gnostics about the mysteries of the various degrees of essence.

Nineteenth-century America produced several prominent advocates of transcendentalism, an intellectual movement with strong gnostic tendencies. Among its proponents were Edward Everett, the president of Harvard University, and his mentor, Ralph Waldo Emerson. But at its core it lacked a core and though Americans were enamored by the lofty verbiage of these intellectuals, we now look back and see how misty it really was. John Updike has compared Emerson's great phrases to "paint that doesn't stick to anything." At the dedication of the cemetery at Gettysburg on November 19, 1963, the principal oration of the day was presented by Edward Everett and it dazzled the audience and especially the eastern newspapers because of its obvious brilliance in the tradition of the transcendentalists. But in fact

Everett's two-hour speech *is* like non-sticking paint. It will put you to sleep when you read it because it lacked concrete substance. It was as if Everett was not aware of the real pathos of the death toll to ordinary families who lost sons and fathers, daughters and brothers to the war between the states. The president of the U.S., Abraham Lincoln, also spoke on that day in what the program called "Remarks." His three-minute speech at Gettysburg put into the soul of America a whole new vision of the meaning of America. His remarks were concrete and personal in sharp contrast to the more abstract and platonic oration of Everett. The President of the United States made clear to every parent or son or daughter or wife who was present that day at Gettysburg that he understood the loss that they felt as this cemetery was dedicated. Lincoln spoke in the rugged and earthy tradition of the Old Testament and New Testament. Everett spoke in the tradition of Plato about shadows and abstract realities.

One of the funniest speeches that Mark Twain ever gave was early in his own career. In it he dared to challenge the platonism of the great Ralph Waldo Emerson himself. The speech was not appreciated either by the audience or the newspaper reporters, and later Mark Twain was especially interested in that rejection that he experienced.

> Now then, I take that speech up and examine it. As I said,
> it arrived this morning, from Boston. I have read it twice,
> and unless I am an idiot, it hasn't a single defect in it from
> the first word to the last. It is just as good as good can be.
> It is smart; it is saturated with humor. There isn't a sug-
> gestion of coarseness or vulgarity in it anywhere. What
> could have been the matter with that house? It is amazing,
> it is incredible, that they didn't shout with laughter, and
> those deities the loudest of them all.

In his speech Twain had imagined Emerson meeting a gold prospecting friend of his in Nevada. The prospector was about to feed his illustrious guest.

> They came here just at dark yesterday evening, and I let

them in of course. Said they were going to the Yosemite. They were a rough lot, but that's nothing: everybody looks rough that travels afoot. Mr. Emerson was a seedy little bit of a chap, redheaded. Mr. Holmes was as fat as a balloon; he weighed as much as three hundred, and had double chins all the way down to his stomach. Mr. Longfellow was built like a prizefighter. His head was cropped and bristly, like as if he had a wig made of hairbrushes. His nose lay straight down his face, like a finger with the end joint tilted up. They had been drinking, I could see that. And what queer talk they used! Mr. Holmes inspected the cabin, then he took me by the buttonhole and says he:

'Through the deep caves of thought
I hear a voice that sings,
Build thee more stately mansions,
O my soul!'

Says I, I can't afford it, Mr. Holmes, and moreover I don't want to.' Blamed if I like it pretty well, either, coming from a stranger, that way. However, I started to get out my bacon and beans, when Mr. Emerson came and looked on awhile, and then he takes me aside by the buttonhole and says:

'Give me agates for my meat;
Give me cantharids to eat;
From air and ocean bring me foods,
From all zones and altitudes.'

Says I, 'Mr. Emerson, if you'll excuse me, this ain't no hotel.' You see it sort of riled me—I warn't use to the ways of littery swells. But I went on a-sweating over my work, and next comes Mr. Longfellow and buttonholes me, and interrupts me. Says he:

'Honor be to Mudjekeewis!
You shall hear how Pau-Pak-Keewis-'

But I broke in, and says I, 'Beg your pardon,
Mr. Longfellow, if you'll be so kind as to hold your yawp
for about five minutes and let me get this grub ready,
you'll do me proud.' Well, sir after they'd filled up I set out
the jug. Mr. Holmes looks at it, and then he fires up all of
a sudden and yells:

'Flash out a stream of blood-red wine!
or I would drink to other days.'

By George, I was getting kind of worked up. I don't deny
it, I was getting kind of worked up. I turns to Mr. Holmes
and says I, 'Looky here, my fat friend, I'm a-
running this shanty, and if the court know herself, you'll
take whisky straight or you'll go dry.' Them's the very
words I said to him. Now, I don't want to sass such famous
littery people, but you see they kind of forced me. There
ain't nothing onreasonable 'bout me: I don't mind a passel
of guests a-treadin' on my tail three or four times, but
when it comes to standing on it it's different, 'and if the
court know herself,' I says, 'you'll take whisky straight or
you'll go dry.' Well, between drinks they'd swell around the
cabin and strike attitudes and spout; and pretty soon they
got out a greasy old deck and went to playing euchre at ten
cents a corner—on trust. I began to notice some pretty suspicious things. Mr. Emerson dealt, looked at his hand,
shook his head, says:

'I am the doubter and the doubt—'

The appearance/reality contrast is present in the humor of irony in the

Bible. It is of the same earthy quality that Mark Twain enjoyed in his spoof of the Harvard transcendentalists. The Hebrew prophets make use of ironic humor to reveal the worthlessness of idolatry. The Old Testament prophet, Habakkuk, humorously instructs his readers to see that for all its sculptural or metallic beauty that an idol is—it's still just an idol. He calls idols "teacher of lies" because the idols that we make to assure successes such as fertility or victory in war, in the end become emblems of a self projected swindle upon ourselves. The very word for idol in Hebrew means "imprint" or "projection." An idol is our own fears, hopes, and expectations projected or imprinted onto an object that somehow is meant to provide the answers we hope for. Habakkuk's humor is ironic and has the visual appeal of what comedians call slapstick comedy.

> What profit is an idol when its maker has shaped it, a metal image, a teacher of lies? For the workman trusts in his own creation when he makes dumb idols! Woe to him who says to a wooden thing, Awake; to a dumb stone, Arise! Can this give revelation? Behold, it is overlaid with gold and silver, and there is no breath at all in it.
> *(Habakkuk 2:18-19)*

As we read this we can see in front of us a careful craftsman hard at work to make the image of wood, stone, gold, silver—he includes these all—and then the worshipper stands back in wonder and pleads for the idol to "Arise!", "Awake!", "Give me a revelation!" but the idol stays quietly dumb; it is fashioned of gold or silver, but worse than dumb the idol has no "breath" in it.

"Breath" is one of the two great Hebrew words for life, the other is "Blood." But an idol has neither living breath or life giving blood. Habakkuk has humorously made it clear than even though the craftsman had the wealth to cover the idol with gold and the strong faith to trust in the idol he or she fashioned yet the result is still the same because the idol is an idol is an idol and nothing more. It appears wise but it is not. What we have here is an ironic Jewish contrast between appearance and reality.

Ironic humor helps those who hear it to recognize that what may appear to us as certain may in fact ironically be less certain what now appears so strong over against the truth of God that is presently under attack is not as strong as it thinks it is. This ironic form of humor becomes the starting place for the consolation promises in the prophecy of Jeremiah.

Jeremiah, the prophet of Judah during the terrible last days of Jerusalem's fall to Babylon, is told by the Lord that his uncle will approach him with a sales pitch to Jeremiah that he should buy from him a field that his uncle owns in the village of Anathoth. Jeremiah is to weigh out the payment for the property and to make certain that the sale is witnessed and that the deed of sale is placed into a sealed jar so that the deed will be safe. What is humorous about this acted out promise is that the Neo-Babylonian armies are actually camped upon that very land as they prepare to destroy Jerusalem and take the people of Jerusalem captive back to Babylon. Why would anyone with any degree of business sense buy property in such a place at such a time? But Jeremiah does just that in one of the most humorous scenes in the Old Testament. Following that sale Jeremiah speaks the unforgettable words of the new covenant book of consolation, "Thus saith the Lord . . . houses and lands shall again be bought in this place you now call a desolation." The purchase is humorous; it is ironic and humorous both at the same time. What could appear so permanently hopeless as does the future prospects of Jerusalem and the towns that surround the great city? Nevertheless, in spite of this appearance, by holy surprise, because of the mighty act of God, the greater reality of God's fulfillment of his promises will happen in God's time toward and in his people. Jeremiah does not play the role of a platonic hero and purchase a spiritual space for spiritual vineyards in the cloud-cuckoo-land future, but he buys a real property where real vineyards grow and where actual land deeds are kept and witnessed. The ironic humor is not set in the contrast between the enduring spiritual and the non-enduring physical but the spiritual and physical are marvelously brought together which is the mark of true spirituality in the Old Testament and New Testament. Jesus makes use of the same kind of ironic humor and with the same objective goal. We look forward not to the immortality of the Spirit but the resurrection of the body. "Because I live you will live also" (Jn 14) are the words of Jesus.

When Jesus is gathering together his twelve disciples one of those disciples, Philip, finds a friend named Nathanael and tells him, (Jn 1:45-51) "We have found him of whom Moses in the Law and also the prophets wrote, Jesus of Nazareth, the son of Joseph." Nathanael replies to Philip, "Can anything good come out of Nazareth?" Philip decides not to argue his case and instead simply says to Nathanael, "Come and see." What happens next is one of the unforgettable encounters with Jesus in the New Testament. "Jesus saw Nathanael coming to him, and said of him, "Behold, an Israelite indeed, in whom is no guile!" Nathanael is amazed that Jesus knew him so well and because of that experience of being known he becomes a believer. Nathanael speaks the strongest confession of faith to be heard from a disciple at that point: "Rabbi, you are the Son of God, you are the King of Israel . . ." Jesus had connected with Nathanael personally and he made the connection in an ironically humorous way. When Philip tells of Jesus to his friend Nathanael, Nathanael objects and says what he really thinks; when Jesus meets Nathanael he says "Behold an Israelite indeed, in whom is no guile." What is ironically funny in this sentence is that the name Israel in the Hebrew language actually means "guile, deception." It was Jacob's deception of his brother Esau that had given Jacob his less than heroic name "Israel," which means "deceiver." Jesus has told an ironic joke about the very name of God's beloved people and in the heart of the humor Jesus has honored Nathanael. Nathanael is an outspoken young man who says what he thinks; he is decidedly not a deceiver.

Jesus understands irony and Jesus humorously offers in his words to Nathanael a new vision for God's people Israel, not the way of guile but the way of openness. In this fulfillment of God's promises it will not be necessary for anyone to steal a blessing away from a brother in order to have a blessing from the God who cannot be deceived by our tricks and never has been as the name of Israel proves. In a simple but dramatic use of the humor of irony with one man named Nathanael the new way is introduced.

Chapter Eleven

The Humor that Heals

ave you known people who are fun to be around, people who seem to draw around themselves situations that are totally enjoyable? When these people are present in a room or place it just seems that funny things happen! They are magnets for laughter; just as some people exude encouragement, love, faith, hope, these folk make us laugh; these are the men or women who have about them an atmosphere of joy and fun.

St. Paul recognized this reality in his description of believers as having the aroma of Christ. He called this reality a "living aroma." The senior devil Screwtape in C.S. Lewis' satirical book *Screwtape Letters* is very concerned when he writes to a junior tempter, Wormwood, about the "patient" who has fallen in love with a young woman. Screwtape alerts Wormwood to the dangers:

> Then, of course, he gets to know this woman's family and whole circle. Could you not see that the very house she lives in is one that he ought never to have entered? The whole place reeks of that deadly odour. The very gardener,

though he has been there only five years, is beginning to acquire it. Even guests, after a weekend visit, carry some of the smell away with them. The dog and the cat are tainted with it. And a house full of the impenetrable mystery…

"It reeks of that deadly odor." Screwtape is describing the aroma of Christ which is a living odor to human beings but a deadly one for the evil one, the devil. Screwtape has the same distrust of the laughter of joy and the laughter of fun.

Fun promotes courage and hope. It always has and that is why families, as much as they need balanced food, strong moral teaching, and spiritual enrichment, also need to play together and to enjoy the humor of fun. As humans we feel a natural attraction toward people who have an instinct for fun. We are nourished when we are around them.

I think Jeremiah, though he is called the weeping prophet of the Old Testament, was really a very funny man. He had many calamities and he tells us in detail about them: he suffered various imprisonments, he was thrown into a pit on one occasion, and he grieved as he witnessed the terrible destruction of his beloved city. These cause Jeremiah to weep as he should and the book of Lamentations is credited to this prophet as he weeps for the destruction of his beloved Jerusalem. But through it all Jeremiah is a humorous man once you get to know him. His "run with horses" answer from God that he records for us is funny. Later he walks into the palace precincts wearing an oxen yoke and that symbolic enactment by the prophet is broad slapstick comedy as much as it is a living parable of judgment; his purchase of the field at Anathoth is wonderfully humorous. It is therefore not a surprise to me that this man is, through it all, able to keep his sanity which humorous people seem to manage to do better than do angry people. The proof of this is even found in his book of Lamentations. Jeremiah weeps for his city and yet he is able to remember the goodness and faithfulness of God. It is this prophet Jeremiah who gives to the whole story of the Bible one of its grandest statements of hope. He begins with sadness but then something better comes into his heart.

Remember my affliction and my bitterness, the wormwood and the gall! My soul continually thinks of it and is bowed down within me. But this I call to mind, and therefore I have hope; The steadfast love of the Lord never ceases, his mercies never come to an end; they are new every morning; great is thy faithfulness, 'The Lord is my portion' says my soul, 'therefore I will hope in him.' The Lord is good to those who wait for him, to the soul that seeks him. It is good that one should wait quietly for the salvation of the Lord.

(Lamentations 3:19-26)

Jonah is another prophet in the Old Testament who as a man is as funny as he is odd. He, like Jeremiah, seems to draw calamity to himself. He is very definite about his resentment toward the great northern empire of Assyria with its capital Nineveh. It is this empire that with merciless cruelty and finality destroyed the northern kingdom of Israel in 720 B.C. We are not surprised that Jonah would resist going as the Lord's messenger to Nineveh. The prophetic book of Jonah tells of this prophet's attempt to sail away from that mandate toward Spain. Through the incredible great fish incident at sea, however, he ends up on shore and Jonah finally agrees to become a prophet of the Lord to Nineveh.

The very best part of the book of Jonah is the humorous statement from the reluctant prophet Jonah, in which he complains bitterly to the Lord following the repentance of Nineveh in response to Jonah's warnings. Their repentance means that the city's population was spared from the destruction they deserved. But instead of joy at such prophetic success, Jonah wants to die.

But it displeased Jonah exceedingly, and he was angry. And he prayed to the Lord and said, 'I pray thee, Lord, is not this what I said when I was yet in my country? That is why I made haste to flee to Tarshish; for I knew that thou are a gracious God and merciful, slow to anger, and abounding in steadfast love, and repentest of evil. Therefore now, O Lord, take my life from me, I beseech thee, for it is better for me to die than to live.'

(Jonah 3:1-3)

How remarkable for the reader of the prophets that one of the greatest statements about the love of God should come in the sour complaint of the Lord's prophet in which Jonah is angry because God is so totally good. "I knew that Thou are a gracious God and merciful, slow to anger, and abounding in steadfast love . . ." This is not a song of joy because of the goodness of God; it is the complaint of a man who wanted to see his enemy punished. Instead of the punishment that this capital city deserves, his enemy is forgiven, and all because God is so generous. "I should have known you would pull a trick like this on me. I had hoped just once you would have not been so eager to forgive, so eager to be merciful." This is a humorous scene that is funny in the totality of the whole event because Jonah is himself so interesting and comic in a very understandable way to those who read his story centuries later.

The New Testament narratives point up people who like Jeremiah and Jonah are interesting to us in that way in which they attract around themselves humorous events and occasions. They seem to be by their nature joyous or like Jonah joyous things happen around them. There is an aroma about them of that "meaningful acceleration" that C. S. Lewis described as the mark of joy. Jesus himself was like this and we know that because one of the charges made against him was that he was not serious enough. Mark's gospel gives a clear picture of this complaint against Jesus:

> And as he sat at table in his house, many tax collectors and sinners were sitting with Jesus and his disciples; for there were many who followed him. And the scribes of the Pharisees, when they saw that he was eating with sinners and tax collectors, said to his disciples, 'Why does he eat with tax collectors and sinners?' And when Jesus heard it, he said to them, 'Those who are well have no need of a physician, but those who are sick; I came not to call the righteous, but sinners.' Now John's disciples and the Pharisees were fasting; and people came and said to him,

'Why do John's disciples and the disciples of the Pharisees fast, but your disciples do not fast?' And Jesus said to them, 'Can the wedding guests fast while the bridegroom is with them? As long as they have the bridegroom with them, they cannot fast. The days will come, when the bridegroom is taken away from them, and then they will fast in that day. No one sews a piece of unshrunk cloth on an old garment; if he does, the patch tears away from it, the new from the old, and a worse tear is made. And no one puts new wine into old wineskins; if he does, the wine will burst the skins, and the wine is lost, and so are the skins; but new wine is for fresh skins.' One Sabbath he was going through the grainfields; and as they made their way his disciples began to pluck heads of grain. And the Pharisees said to him, 'Look, why are they doing what is not lawful on the Sabbath?'

(Mark 2:15-24)

In another place Jesus himself reflects on the difference between himself and the more serious John the Baptist.

To what then shall I compare the men of this generation, and what are they like? They are like children sitting in the market place and calling to one another, 'We piped to you, and you did not dance; we wailed, and you did not weep.' For John the Baptist has come eating no bread and drinking no wine; and you say, 'He has a demon.' The Son of man has come eating and drinking; and you say, 'Behold, a glutton and a drunkard, a friend of tax collectors and sinners!' Yet wisdom is justified by all her children.

(Luke 7:31-35)

For those who were disciples of Jesus of Nazareth it was not a hard duty station but a series of surprises and adventures that were as much fun events and experiences as they were important training events in the lives of the disciples that Jesus was preparing to send into the world. They would need the energy of joy to carry on in the mandate that will be theirs.

Most of the miracles of Jesus are the miracles of compassion, but two are clearly celebrative miracles. The sign at the Cana wedding is one such miracle. The other one is on the Lake of Tiberius—totally celebrative and even fun, though it has a good scare in the middle of it. Jesus instructs his disciples after the great sign of the feeding of the 5,000 to cross the lake from the north shore to the small harbor at Caperneum. Matthew, Mark and John all narrate this unforgettable experience.

> Then he made the disciples get into the boat and go before him to the other side, while he dismissed the crowds. And after he had dismissed the crowds, he went up on the mountain by himself to pray. When evening came, he was there alone, but the boat by this time was many furlongs distant from the land, beaten by the waves; for the wind was against them. And in the fourth watch of the night he came to them, walking on the sea. But when the disciples saw him walking on the sea, they were terrified, saying, 'It is a ghost!' And they cried out for fear. But immediately he spoke to them, saying, 'Take heart, it is I; have no fear.'
>
> *(Matthew 14:22-27)*

This is a sign of pure and simple joy with a fright that intensifies the hilarity. Jesus' disciples needed this sign and it was a sign just for them. It is fun, adventurous, and highly personal for each man. It has fright as a key first ingredient because the disciples on the lake at night were worried about the strong winds. If that were not enough they also had to worry about seeing a ghost, but the event ends in the excitement of their most unforgettable night on this lake which they knew so well. Readers of the New Testament are required to make an interpretive decision about such New Testament scenes as this one. Did this event actually happen as the gospel writers tell the story? If it did, then this event on the lake is a sign given by Jesus Christ himself for reasons he has. Or a reader may wonder if this scene is a story of faith/grace told by early church writers to encourage the faith of we who later read the account? If we chose the second interpretive stance then this scene and other miracle stories in the New Testament are signs given to us by the early church to encourage our faith in Jesus as the mighty Son of God. It is my conviction both for textual as well as theological reasons that we should rightly interpret this scene as a sign given by Jesus himself. This means that the scene on the lake, as remarkable as it is, happened in the way the gospel writers tell it, and the event therefore shocked the disciples as much as it shocks us. I hold this interpretive understanding for the following reasons. First it is the way the narrative is written by the gospel writers themselves. Matthew, Mark, Luke and John have shown to their readers that as writers they are able to draw the distinction between parable and event. Parables which our Lord tells are stories meant to inspire faith. Each writer of the gospels preserves the parables as stories. These writers also know how to narrate events which include all the details that are essential to event narrative. My second reason is a fundamental theological reason. Jesus in the gospels is known by what he says and what he does, what Karl Barth describes as the inseparable mixture of "word and work". These two cannot and must not be separated from each other. New Testament theology must not permit such a separation. This means that the love of Jesus Christ is not only the theoretical message content of what Jesus said but in equal importance the love of Jesus is found in what Jesus did. Love is event that happens as much as it is verbal and theological idea. The miracles of Jesus and the supreme miracle at the cross and empty grave are all inevitably united as parts of one whole portrait of Jesus who is known to us by word and act. The word and the act are not divided nor should we divide them.

My third reason is a whimsical one. If this scene and other miracles of Jesus in the gospels are signs given to us by the early church writers then it means that the very best parts of the gospel, the parts that children instinctively love best of all with the miracles of the marvelous are stories written by the early church novelists who have written the gospels for us. That interpretive guideline leaves a few epigrams and sayings that we will allow for the authentic record of Jesus. Years later a few "scholars" will meet in Eugene, Oregon as a "Jesus Seminar" and they will tell us which epigrams are on the approved list. This group of New Testament interpreters will have periodic elections among themselves to vote on the allowibility of New Testament texts. Most miracle texts will be excluded in these elections. They will allow a few appropriately enlightened epigrams to the Jesus in their revised New Testament. This means that the most exciting parts of the gospels become the "fictional" stories told by the early church in an attempt to show those who read the New Testament what God's love would be like if it were practical and at human scale. What an affront this is to the texts of the Bible from every standard rule of literary criticism! It is an affront also to the common sense of any ordinary reader of the texts themselves. The better rule is to struggle with the text as it stands in the document rather than to etherize the parts that seem too dangerous or lively.

Pascal put it best, "A king knows to speak of power, a rich man knows how to speak about wealth and God knows how to speak about God." Jesus Christ does not need the early church writers to make him relevant, or to show what his love is really like, or to show what is the joy that radiates from his character. Jesus can speak for himself. Jesus knows how to touch those who have leprosy. He knows how to bless children. It is not an ancient church novelist trying to show us what love would be like if it were personal; it is Jesus himself giving to us signs of his character and of our worth. Jesus knows how to rescue from embarrassment the bridegroom at a wedding when the wine had failed, and Jesus does it with style. Jesus knows how to walk on the water; and he actually did it because his crew of trainees needed that concrete, hilarious, dangerous, unforgettable moment in the middle of the night on a famous lake. Peter needed to try to walk on the water too. The fact is that Jesus is exciting to be around and here is one more concrete instance that shows it to us.

Peter is also a humorous man to be around and there is no question that Peter draws humorous incidents around him. His comments have a comic edge to them, even the ones that he regrets.

At the lake incident it is Peter who asks Jesus if he can try out walking on the water too. We are grateful to Matthew for including that P.S. to this incident.,

> And Peter answered him, 'Lord, if it is you, bid me come
> to you on the water.' He said, 'Come.' So Peter got out of

the boat and walked on the water and came to Jesus; but
when he saw the wind, he was afraid, and beginning to sink
he cried out, 'Lord, save me.' Jesus immediately reached
out his hand and caught him, saying to him, 'O man of little faith, why did you doubt?' And when they got into the
boat, the wind ceased. And those in the boat worshiped
him, saying, 'Truly you are the Son of God.'

(Matthew 14:28-33)

We enjoy Peter's impetuousness and the way he is like a magnet for
such comic moments.

When I was a seminary student at Princeton Seminary a fellow student
who became my best friend in the ministry was very much like Peter in the
way that funny things always seemed to happen around him and to him. We
who loved him as a friend gradually collected our list of Dick Jacobson stories. On one occasion four of us were members of a gospel team leading
worship at an historic Presbyterian Church in Lambertville, NJ. Dick,
though a typical southern Californian UCLA man, wanted to appear very
"eastern" and proper in the morning worship service as he
carried out the one single part of the service that was assigned to him. He
was to read the Old Testament lesson. Dick stood before the huge pulpit
Bible, paused a moment, smiled warmly to the congregation and then said,
"Let us hear God's word from the Old Testament lesson as we listen to that
most beloved of all texts in the Old Testament from the prophet Isaiah,
Isaiah 53:1-10." We on the team were surprised by Dick's florid introduc-
tion to the reading because our training had been to simply say, "The Old
Testament text for today is Isaiah 53:1-10. Let us hear the word of God." We
all wondered why Dick had added that line about "most beloved text in all
of Isaiah." But the funny part happened next. He reached down and before
him was the great pulpit Bible of that historic church. Dick opened the
Bible and found Isaiah and then began to turn pages. It seemed like an endless journey through pages as he moved from page to page first one way
and then in the other direction. We could see sweat drops on his forehead.
Finally he just began to read a random ten verses from a random chapter of
Isaiah. The pulpit Bible was numbered in Roman numerals and Dick could

not find 53 which only a Latin student would know as LIII. He then regretted his grand statement about "most beloved text." We on the team had one more Dick Jacobson story to add to our list. But he was not a victim of our jokes for long, and like Peter he could come up with his own jokes to even the playing field. About a week later I was the leader in an early morning Bible study group to which several of us belonged and during that early morning study I was asked a question about an Old Testament incident. I answered the question quite certain I was correct but a university freshman who was in the group with those of us who were seminary students pointed up that my answer was incorrect and with excellent Sunday School training under his belt he proved it with an Old Testament citation. It was an embarrassment for me since I was supposed to be the leader of that study that I thought included less informed university students. After all, they were the learners and we seminary students were their mentors. Later that day as my seminary friends and I were entering the seminary dining commons to eat Dick whispered in my ear in mock seriousness: "Stay out of the Old Testament." That wonderfully funny put down became the standard greeting for my circle of Princeton friends that has lasted to this day. At a gathering following my friend Dick Jacobson's funeral, as we grieved for the untimely death of that great man, we told Dick Jacobson stories and laughed. He drew humor to himself like Peter and yet not really as a victim of jokes "on him" but as a good man who was just fun to be around.

On the day of Pentecost an amazing and miraculous happening took place—a reversal of the Tower of Babel scene in the Old Testament. As the disciples were praying together the gift of dramatic communication happened and the citizens from different parts of the Mediterranean world who were in Jerusalem heard the disciples praising God in their own native languages. The large crowd that was drawn by this gift of communication phenomena could only think of one way to describe the joyous event they were witnessing. "These men are drunk on new wine." It is Peter who as leader of the apostles then stands up to speak and he decides to begin the first sermon at the occasion of the birth of the Christian church with a humorous remark.

"These men are not drunk; you know it is only 9 a.m. in the morning." The humorous point of the remark by Peter is that even those who are regular drinkers don't get drunk at 9 in the morning. Peter is a superb communicator. He does not waste time with denials of the drunkenness accusation; he does not divert the argument with statements about the disciples' committment to moderation or abstinence. He does not offer proofs of their sobriety. Peter does not waste time on the cynical drunkenness accusation because he has a larger goal and he makes use of humor to refocus the crowd in the special way that humor is able to do. He refocused his listeners' attention toward the center. His humor enabled him to bypass meaningless side questions.

Peter had himself experienced that refocusing at a critical moment in his life when he was obsessed with the grief of his own denial of Jesus. Our Lord refocused Peter at the lake of Galilee by a means that was humorous, strong and tender all at the same time. Because of this experience of his own Peter is now himself able to offer the same gift to people he is called upon to serve and to lead.

Chapter Twelve

The Humor of Argument

Men and women who have a sense of humor are always at an advantage in arguments; this is true in politics as it is in business. It is true also when families argue, and in the debates that happen in matters of faith.

The humor of Winston Churchill became part of the folklore of the war years. But his humor was not only a self-serving leadership weapon he was able to use in political controversy. He made use of humor to keep hope alive in his endangered country during the battle of Britain. It became a vital ideological part of the fatal argument between his country as they fought against the Axis powers. When the German Führer, Adolf Hitler, would make a speech, it was usually answered by the British Prime Minister in Parliament. Churchill was the master of the eloquent rejoinder and humor was always a part of the argument. The story is told that in one speech Hitler had boasted that Germany would wring England's neck like a chicken. In Parliament on the next day Churchill had found his mark in the humorless and vain Hitler. "Herr Hitler announces that he wants to wring

England's neck like a chicken. Let him try but he will find out that England is some chicken and some neck." What a superb English language joke! It may be difficult to translate into German but every English speaker knows exactly what it means. The argumentative humor of England's Prime Minister was the subject of many stories. Karsh of Ottawa had won the permission to photograph Churchill who only grudgingly agreed to sit for the photo session. Karsh had no success getting the exact pose of the great man that in his mind would capture the essential spirit in his subject. He tells in his own memoirs that he captured what became the most famous photo of Churchill with a surprise. He suddenly grabbed Churchill's cigar and took it out of his mouth and he snapped his photo of the humorist Churchill at that moment of the surprise when the joke had been pulled on Churchill. Karsh caught the marvelous scowl of Sir Winston Churchill.

Humor not only connects people it also advances the argument that is underway between people and between ideas. The argumentative role of humor is important to understand. This means that humor not only disarms pompous statements and shows their foolish side but the same humor if wisely managed will make its own teaching point. "Some chicken … some neck" plays a two-fold role. It dares to take hold of what was meant by Hitler in his example. Hitler had intended it to be a terrifying prelude of the deadly future that the helpless England faced as Germany prepared for what was an inevitable crossing of the English Channel. It was intended to demoralize the population but Churchill's "Some chicken, some neck!" takes a firm grip on the terror of Hitler's statement as if to say, "Is that the best you can do to scare us, Herr Hitler? We know what your plans are, but it is you who should be afraid when you take on the English chicken and the English neck. We are the very last chicken you will ever meet." The whole context of terror has been thrown into question by the humorous statement of the Prime Minister and the roar of laughter in the House of Parliament. We are not so sure just who is on the defensive now. It has been achieved by humor, and the tough courage of England too.

Franklin D. Roosevelt was one of America's most humorous presidents. His jaunty, infectious smile added to a totally unique voice and a masterful choice of words that made his speeches and fireside chats very important road markers of encouragement during the confusing years of the 1930s and the wartime years of World War II. When war had already broken out in Europe, FDR made no secret of his own support for Great Britain and the European nations that were then under attack by the Axis coalition. He was aware more than anyone in America of the awful danger to the world of the total collapse of England in the face of the growing Axis power on the continent. FDR was determined to send military help to England but he was faced with strong isolationist forces in the Congress of the U.S. The American constitution mandates that Congress must approve federal budgets and the federal expenditure of money, therefore aid to England was not in the President's power except for modest emergency expenditure powers that the President could effect by presidential signature. In the face of strong isolationist opposition to U.S. involvement, FDR and his Secretary of State Cordell Hull created a grand myth to bypass the opposition he faced in Congress. He called his plan to provide immediate and massive military assistance to Great Britain (and later to the USSR) *lend-lease*. FDR was able at an all-important Presidential press conference to defuse congressional opposition to U.S. expenditure of funds for what many then called the "war in Europe." He stated that what he had authorized and now wanted Congress to also endorse was only the lending and leasing of supplies to England for which the U.S. would naturally expect repayment. His most brilliant statement in that press conference was a humorous illustration that he invented to explain the basic concept of lend-lease. He said, "If your neighbor's house was on fire and you had a hose would you not lend him your hose to help him put out the fire? And when the fire is over you would expect him to return it." In the harsh hour of England's house fire the American president told an ordinary story that every ordinary person could relate to and he ended it with a humorous postscript, "We expect our neighbor to return the hose when the fire is over." The humor in the PS is obvious. There could be no returning of the lifeline of supplies that were loaded on the vast Atlantic convoys then headed to the island country that was holding out against Germany. His humorous illustration advanced the argument, but in strict terms, the logic defied any careful accounting; how do you "lend" a jeep or troop carrier? And how do you return it? But no rejoinders from isolationist solons could stop America's growing involvement with the fire of Europe. Americans saw the fire and they wanted to help put it out.

Jesus was a humorous teacher and Jesus made skillful use of the humor of argument; he understood the humor of argument, its advantages and its limits. In the Sermon on the Mount Jesus argues against wrong ideas about prayer that had sabotaged the simplicity and amateur nature of prayer. Prayer had become more of an art form than an amateur event, especially from 150 B.C. onward, with the Pharisees' insistence on precise definition even in the language of prayer. Such sects as the Essenes specialized their prayers to an even more demanding level than the Pharisees, particularly in their concerns for ritual and Sabbath purity. Prayers were infected by a strong emphasis on the battle against the enemies of God's true people, especially foreigners. This means that the prayers found in the Dead Sea scrolls are more like war cries, anti-foreign diatribes, and formulas for ritual cleansings than they are the language of friendship with God. The joyous and realistic prayers that are found in the Psalms and the prophets had been forgotten and replaced by highly technical, highly self-conscious, and above all the form of technical prayers that were the property of an elite group of technical religious specialists. It was therefore expected of a Rabbi by the time of the first century that he would teach his followers a special collection of proper and correct prayers which could then be used for the different occasions of life as needed. Jesus breaks with that whole system and expectation in the way that he teaches about prayer. He returns prayer to its older amateur status as the language between friends. He allows prayers to be what a man or woman, boy or girl would blurt out from their heart either in praise or in worry, intercession or in complaint. Prayer does not need to be an artistic work of art because, like all other communication, prayer employs the language of normal language. Jesus teaches about prayer to his disciples in the Sermon on the Mount (Mt 5, 6, 7). Our Lord makes very skillful use of humor to advance this important amature argument against ingrained technical patterns. We watch how Jesus makes this argument in the Sermon on the Mount:

> And when you pray, you must not be like the hypocrites;
> for they love to stand and pray in the synagogues and in the
> streets, that they may be praised by men. Truly, I say to

you, they have received their reward. But when you pray, go into your room and shut the door and pray to your Father who is in secret; and your Father who sees in secret will reward you.

(Matthew 6:5-6)

Two images that Jesus creates are visually humorous, ". . . Stand and pray . . . at the street corners, that they may be seen by other people." The humor is obvious. Here is a person who we thought was praying to God and yet he is making sure that he looks right and is seen in his moment of devotion at the right place by the right people. It is the macabre humor of a person getting dressed to attend a funeral and then making certain that he or she looks just right so that the people who are there will be impressed. We laugh at such misplaced priorities but it makes the point that the dress conscious mourner has turned mourning into an art form whereas it should have been a simple human time of vulnerability.

Jesus also advances his argument against the endless repetition of intercession with his humorous comment,

And in praying do not heap up empty phrases as the Gentiles do; for they think that they will be heard for their many words. Do not be like them, for your Father knows what you need before you ask him.

(Matthew 6:7-8)

One empty phrase added to another empty phrase does not increase volume in any substantive sense. Here is a very funny and yet tragic picture that Jesus has painted for his disciples; it is of a person who busily adds sentences together in a desperate attempt to say so much that the volume of the words will ensure a successful hearing of the prayer. Prayers to such deities as are found in the Greek-Roman mystery religion idols, might conceivably be helped by repetition. Isis or Artemus or Aphrodite or even Zeus will need many prayers but the prayers won't work because no amount of repetitious devotion will help if no one is listening. In sharp contrast if someone can hear and cares to hear then even the faintest cry for help is enough.

Jesus also warns against all emptiness in language. One summer, during our family vacation when my son was in high school, he and I practically drove the family out of their minds with "deep thoughts" that we dreamed up. Especially on occasions when unsuspecting friends were in our house, we would try out a deep thought. Whatever I or Jon would say, the other would then say, "You know that is very deep, what you just said" our guests would look baffled because somehow they missed the profoundness but we made it a policy to never explain the depth. One of our best thoughts was this. One day Jon said to me, "You know, dad, people often disappoint you, but then again they also let you down." I told him that that was a very deep thought in my opinion. But try to imagine prayers that are built upon a large collection of such deep thoughts and we then see the wonderful humor of Jesus at work teaching us about the meaning of prayer. No deep thoughts are needed: just say what you mean and mean what you say.

Jesus also makes use of humor to advance his argument about the proper role in a disciple's life of such self denial acts of piety as fasting.

> And when you fast, do not look dismal, like the hypocrites,
> for they disfigure their faces that their fasting may be seen
> by men. Truly, I say to you, they have received their
> reward. But when you fast, anoint your head and wash
> your face, that your fasting may not be seen by men but by
> your Father who is in secret; and your Father who sees in
> secret will reward you.
>
> *(Matthew 6:16-18)*

There are some people who will contort their faces to let those who are around them know how much they are personally sacrificing to fulfill their fasting goal. We immediately see the humor in this portrayal by Jesus as well. I have been at dinners with dieters and devoted health fooders who make it a public relations part of their own health regime to impress those who have the misfortune to be around them during one of their lectures about the difficulty of the fast or special diet which they themselves chose. These people are funny when they are not obnoxious. Jesus moves beyond the humorous reflection upon those who "make a bad face" when they fast as an act of piety, and he goes forward to make the point that those who fast should wash their faces and carry on the fast in a healthy way. Jesus, by means of humor, makes a teaching point in a very clear way that the non-healthy fasting of anorexia or bulimia in no way can become a part of God's plan for the life of a disciple. Every fast must be healthy; it is not an art form to be seen as an end in itself but fasting, like prayer and gifts given to the poor, should flow out of the normal healthy life of faith in God.

St. Paul makes very effective use of the humor of argument in his development of major teaching themes. In the beginning of the letter to the Corinthians Paul is alarmed by the factionalism of the Corinthians and he tells them that through visitors who have come recently to Ephesus where he is now living he has heard that the Corinthian church has divided into parties around such heroes as Peter and Apollos and even Paul himself. Paul's approach to this crisis makes use of ironic humor in the services of his argument against the factionalism. He writes, "Is Christ divided? Was Paul crucified for you? Or were you baptized in the name of Paul?" (1 Cor 1:13). The Corinthians would smile at this humorous line. Paul is not the one who has deserved the right to become in any sense a center focusing point for a believer. It would be ridiculous to think of a baptismal service where a believer or a believer's son or daughter would be subjected to such a ceremony, "I baptize you, Mary Elizabeth, in the name of Paul the Father, Paul the Son and Paul the Holy Spirit." The apostle humorously mocks this possibility concerning himself. Notice that Paul does not make Apollos or Peter the object of this humorous argument. Paul tells the joke on himself and it enables him to make the much more important theological point with the Corinthians that only Jesus Christ deserves to stand at the living center of their loyalty. The proof of this centeredness of Christ is in the cross and the sign is baptism.

St. Paul like his Lord has carried this vital teaching forward by the skillful use of humor.

Chapter Thirteen
Salty Humor

Humor has a pastoral role to play in the lives of people especially at the times of extreme pressure and the times of fear. Pastoral humor will then become an encouragement to the oppressed and the frightened. Humor's pastoral role is to soften the brittle edge that develops interpersonally when tensions escalate for whatever reasons. The humorist is able through humor or comedy to name the cause of the tension but with just enough indirectness that a highly stressed man or woman is enabled to face and handle that tension build up that is happening within them with all of its dangerous side effects. Humor helps them to see the stress and its sources without as much defensiveness as if they were directly confronted about how tense they appear. The humorist does not directly confront a highly pressured man or woman with the plain statement of the truth of the matter: "You are a very tense person"; "Calm down; you are far too uptight about this matter"; "Don't be so frightened"; or the statment can be stated as a direct question, "Why are you so negative?"; "Why are you such a scaredy-cat?" These straightforward statements and questions may be true but they are only rarely helpful in frightening situations. There are only a few settings in which direct confrontations are able to result in producing less cause for panic and less fear. Human beings need more than a rebuke to take away nervousness and to reduce panic even if the rebuke states a truth.

If the direct confrontation is to actually have a positive result it needs to be matched with strong and reliable leadership that is able to offer a reason against the fear or situation that causes the stress. A physician in an emergency room can effect a reduction in panic by a direct command because the physician is doing something to help and the patient knows that actual help is on its way. Jesus Christ was able to rebuke fear for an even stronger reason. He tells his disciples in the Thursday evening discourse (Jn 16:33), "In the world you will have intense pressure. Be not afraid for I have overcome the world." His direct promise is supported by his character and his authority. On the first day of the week, following the dreadful day of Friday, the disciples are in hiding in Jerusalem and the women go to the tomb early in the day. They are terrified to find the tomb open, but an angel speaks to them. The angel's words are "Be not afraid . . . Jesus whom you seek is not here, he is risen." This direct confrontation fulfills the promise Jesus had given on Thursday eve and is helpful now on the first day because of the second half of the sentence they first heard on Thursday. It is not that the brave women who have dared to go to the tomb of Jesus early in the morning are being scolded for their fear. Nevertheless their real fear needs to be addressed and the angel directly confronts the fear with good news. It is not that these women will never again experience fear, but they will never face fears with the same dread as before.

There are times when a confrontation that is plain, direct and blunt is the very shock that a man or woman, boy or girl may need in order to clear the air or reduce panic. But when the crisis is not obvious and clear cut then the rule is that we human beings must offer warnings with careful and wise restraint. The only exception to that rule is in the case of a clear and present emergency when all rules cease and we do what must be done and then hope for the best. At such a crisis moment we do not worry about hurt feelings or defensiveness issues. If a car is bearing down on an unwary pedestrian it is proper and essential to shout out a warning, "Look out!" or

"Stand back!" But there are few emergency moments of such traumatic intensity that qualify for stark emergency bluntness, and, moreover, it is a very great mistake to treat non-emergencies as if they were emergencies. If we cry "wolf" more than two times when there is no wolf then those who are around us will always downgrade every warning we pronounce. This is a basic principle of human communication. I know an economist who has made it his specialty to warn people against what he predicts will be the impending financial collapse of the American economy. His problem is that his warnings (with his added advice that investors therefore buy gold and store water in large containers) have gone wrong for him and for those who have taken his "emergency" advice to heart. A friend of his humorously summed up this economist's mistake, "As an economic analyst he has predicted ten of the last two recessions." Those who warn and those who are able to effectively confront require unusual wisdom and considerable interpersonal skills; they must possess proven good will and they must be recognized for their pertinent qualifications. We must earn the right to confront another human being whomever they are. In T. S. Eliot's play, *The Cocktail Party,* the two characters Edward and Lavinia are very controlling aristocrats and apparently self-assured in their personal demeanor until they meet up with the central character in the play, Prof. O'Reilly, the psychiatrist. In the play they are speaking with him in his office since they, as independently wealthy and avant-garde moderns, are able to afford a private psychiatrist, and their enjoyment in having their own therapist is settling in upon the arrogant couple. Then, by surprise, the psychiatrist shocks them with the blunt statement that what they need is "salvation" and not therapy. Edward stands to his feet in one of the most electrifying scenes in the play. He says angrily, "We have not come here to be insulted." O'Reilly answers without any emotion, "Sit down, Edward and Lavinia, you have come to the place where the word insult has no meaning." Now the air is cleared! I can still remember seeing *The Cocktail Party* in San Francisco when I was an undergraduate at UC Berkeley in which Vincent Price played the role of O'Reilly. Eliot is a literary hero of mine and I remember the audience roaring with applause at this turning point scene of the play. We enjoy such success of bluntness and direct confrontation in which truth is made vivid and unmistakably clear, even painfully so, to characters as smug as Edward and Livena, but we can point to very few such successes in our own interpersonal relationships. Parents who major in scolding their children usually raise up highly defensive sons and daughters who must learn how to deflect the constant warnings and emergency statements that come from their too concerned parents. They learn such skills in order to handle their parents; unfortunately those deflection skills often actually do harm to the youth who masters such tactics. How many teenagers end up shivering at a baseball game because they shrugged off their mother's emergency warning, "If you don't take your heavy coat you'll catch pneumonia"? The warning was earnest and caring though it was overstated and non-scientific, but most of all it had become entangled with control and independence issues which made it hard for a son or daughter to really hear the truth or wisdom in the warning.

The strategy of humor is indirect rather than direct. The humorist creates a story alongside of our story and, by means of the story that comes along side of our daily life situations, we are indirectly able to see the danger for what it is; the intensity level is reduced by the very indirectness and in the reduction the terror factor of what we fear is also reduced. Seattle experienced economic recession and high unemployment during the 1980s; there were sharp cutbacks at Boeing Aircraft and many engineers who chose to stay with Boeing were forced to move to Kansas or Louisiana where Boeing still had jobs to offer them. Everyone suffered from this recession but one humorist in Seattle said the fear outloud on a billboard, "Will the last person who leaves please put out the lights?" The people of Seattle did not enjoy the recession but they did enjoy photographing this sign and telling each other about it. This kind of humor is like the collection of "El Niño" jokes that are becoming a current part of modern folk humor. These humorous jokes in which just about everything is blamed on "El Niño" helps us to face crises in a way that enables us to see the danger but then in the laughter to realize that it could be worse; also in the laughter that others enjoy with us we see the crises together and there is encouragement in knowing a fact, even a hard one, together with others.

Jesus makes use of humor for pastoral reasons, as do his disciples after him. The Roman oppression of the Jewish nation was a hard reality. It involved the highly efficient Roman methods of local governance mixed together with the most powerful and successful military apparatus that the ancient world had ever encountered. Certain groups within Jewish culture, in their restlessness to be free from the Roman control of their land, had tried to find ways to oppose Roman rule. Each of these attempts sputtered with various insurrection challenges and came to a terrible, final catastrophe at 70 A.D. when Rome crushed the Jews and destroyed the city of Jerusalem. As a final insult Rome even renamed the city of peace by a new name, Aeolia Capitolina. During the ministry of Jesus there were several times when the fear of, and resentment toward, the Romans became the focus of questions that Jesus was asked to address as a rabbi among the people. Luke narrates one of those instances to us. A rabbi, as a teacher of the law, is expected to have wise answers to hard questions, therefore those who were intent on discrediting Jesus would be expected to ask him the hard questions hoping that he would err in his answers. The Broadway musical *Fiddler on the Roof,* which tells the story of a Jewish community settled within Russia on the eve of the Bolshevik Revolution, offers an example of hard, even impossible, questions that are posed to the rabbi just to see how well he is able to answer the question. These hard questions become a test of the rabbi more than a quest for answers to troubling questions. In the opening "Tradition" song of *Fiddler,* the beloved rabbi is introduced by Tevye the Milkman. As Tevye narrates and sings in that opening theme song a young man with an impudent voice asks the rabbi, "Rabbi, is there a proper greeting for the Czar?" There is a twitter of anticipation in the background as the people wait for the Rabbi's answer. Finally after a moment of silence he speaks, "Yes, there is—O Lord keep the Czar (a few seconds pause and the then the rest of the sentence) —far from us." The crowd roars its approval and the song continues. The humor in the rabbi's reply was in a pause just after the word czar.

Jesus, the Rabbi, is asked a very hard question that brings to the surface the anger and fears of the people toward the Roman power; the question is also a test of Jesus as a rabbi.

> They asked him, 'Teacher, we know that you speak and
> teach rightly, and show no partiality, but truly teach the
> way of God. Is it lawful for us to give tribute to Caesar, or

not?' But he perceived their craftiness, and said to them, 'Show me a coin. Whose likeness and inscription has it?' They said, 'Caesar's.' He said to them, 'Then render to Caesar the things that are Caesar's, and to God the things that are God's.' And they were not able in the presence of the people to catch him by what he said; but marveling at his answer they were silent.

(Luke 20:21-26)

Most interpreters of this famous text are impressed by the skill of Jesus in defending himself from those who are attempting to trip him up with their very difficult question. They recognize the question and Jesus' answer as an example of the use of humor by Jesus to reply to the kinds of hard questions that are often used by folk who want to see how a leader, as a person of publicly announced convictions, will answer such questions. But Jesus has a larger goal than to win at a rabbi testing exercise. He used the rich humor of the coin with its face of Caesar to pastorally achieve a greater and higher ground for those who hear him and watch him. Jesus puts the face of Caesar together with the fears of the people about a power so great that it is able to tax them and to order their daily life. He places both the face of Caesar and the people who fear him onto the larger stage of the kingly reign of God. Give Caesar's coins to him; that is a very small thing to do—after all the coin belongs to him anyway; Give to God what belongs to God; that is a much greater thing to do. It is the difference in size that has a pastorally encouraging result for those who listened that day, and that difference in size still continues to encourage us today. Caesar has power to compel taxes, but God deserves our honor because of a greater power. The humor of Jesus has diminished the extent of the threat from Caesar. Jesus has taught and encouraged and challenged his listeners without scolding the people for their fears, nor does he scold them for bowing under the pressures of Rome and paying their taxes. We now know that Jesus is fully aware of what we are up against on a day to day basis. Jesus knows about taxes, about the tyranny of economic control systems that are frightening because they are so gradual, so inevitable, and so efficient. But God's kingly reign is greater still.

The importance of this pastoral humor is that it creates a story along side of our story and the second story encourages those who hear it to think through for themselves what are the deeper meanings. In this way, humor honors the ones who hear the story and grants a freedom with inner dignity which transcends the fears that press in upon every human being. During the ministry of Jesus of Nazareth his most powerful use of this pastoral humor of analogy occurred during his first journey to Jerusalem.

According to John's narration Jesus challenged the moneychangers in the temple on his first visit to Jerusalem.

> The Passover of the Jews was at hand, and Jesus went up to Jerusalem. In the temple he found who were selling oxen and sheep and pigeons, and the moneychangers at their business. And making a whip of cords, he drove them all, with the sheep and oxen, out of the temple; and he poured out the coins of the moneychangers and overturned their tables. And he told those who sold the pigeons, 'Take these things away; you shall not make my Father's house a house of trade.' His disciples remembered that it was written, 'Zeal for thy house will consume me.' The Jews then said to him, 'What sign have you to show us for doing this?'
>
> *(John 2:13-18)*

The other gospel writers note that later on in Jesus' ministry, on Palm Sunday, Jesus again chases moneychangers out of the temple. I am not surprised that they are back at their tables in this profitable institution that the Sadducees have permitted and for which they are given profitable commissions by the moneychangers. The Pharisees opposed this invasion of the temple precincts but, since they did not have a majority in the Sanhedrin, they could not prevail in this concern. When Jesus challenged the moneychangers and they ran from his sudden disruption of their tables it is interesting to note in both John's account and later in the synoptic gospels that the people at large and the most respected leaders of the people do not say to Jesus, "Stop what you are doing!" The reason they did not is that most of them agreed with Jesus' challenge of the moneychangers. The crowds that watched enjoyed the witty and unforgettable statement that Jesus made on that highly charged occasion: "It is written, my house shall be a house of prayer, but you have made it a den of robbers" (Lk 19:46). This humorous analogy helps ordinary people to see a corrupt institution for what it is and, at the same moment, to see a picture of what the temple is according to God's intention. Jesus skillfully combines the pastoral statement of the prophet Isaiah, "My house shall be called a house of prayer for all peoples" (Isa 56:7) with the salty statement of the prophet Jeremiah, "Has this house, which is called by my name, become a den of robbers …?" (Jer 7:11).

John's account tells of a question that the crowd then asks him following his bold move against the moneychangers.

Jesus answers their question with another humorous analogy that is both cryptic and also unforgettable, "Destroy this temple and in three days I will raise it up." Those who hear him cannot understand any analogy that is present in our Lord's words. They hear him literally and that is how they respond.

> The Jews then said, 'It has taken forty-six years to build this temple, and will you raise it up in three days?' But he spoke of the temple of his body. When therefore he was raised from the dead, his disciples remembered that he had said; this; and they believed the scripture and the word which Jesus has spoken.
>
> *(John 2:20-22)*

His words remained fixed in their memory, however, and we need this narrative by John to understand the charges that are later made against Jesus during his trial before the High Priest. Matthew tells us of that charge.

"Now the chief priests and the whole council sought false testimony against Jesus that they might put him to death, but they found none, though many false witnesses came forward. At last two came forward and said, 'This fellow said, 'I am able to destroy the temple of God, and to build it in three days.' And the high priest stood up and said, 'Have you no answer to

make? What is it that these men testify against you?; But Jesus was silent."
(Mt 26:59-63a)

The people remembered what he had said. At the time of the crucifixion Mark narrates that the crowd also taunted Jesus with these same words:

> And it was the third hour, when they crucified him. And
> the inscription of the charge against him read, 'The King
> of the Jews.' And with him they crucified two robbers, one
> on his right and one on his left. And those who passed by
> derided him, wagging their heads, and saying, 'Aha! You
> who would destroy the temple and build it in three days,
> save yourself, and come down from the cross!' So also the
> chief priests mocked him to one another with the scribes,
> saying, 'He saved others; he cannot save himself.'
>
> *(Mark 15:25-31)*

The analogy is powerful because the temple has such emotional as well as spiritual significance for the people. Jesus, in a hidden way, has given by indirect means a sign of hope to his disciples which later they would be able to understand and treasure. It is like the "sign of Jonah" that Jesus also tells of in explaining who he is. The very thought of the great temple of Jerusalem being destroyed and then rebuilt in three days is so startling that it becomes one of the unforgettable sayings of Jesus even though the promise of victory for Jesus himself is totally cryptic in the saying, as John notes in his account. At the beginning we see the humor at one level, and later on we see the full humor at a profounder level. The thought of it! A temple that took 36 years to build falling down and then amazingly reconstructed in only three days? We would say of such a feat, "How very strange! How very amazing! How funny to see such a thing happen!" The disciples enjoyed their Lord's statement at one level when they first heard it. They know of his power to heal and of his power to turn water to wine but now this! For them it was one more example, a humorous one at that, of the amazing things that Jesus could do and therefore at that level the statement was an encouragement sign for them. Later on, on Easter Sunday, they would know the whole truth which would give the sign its greater and permanent meaning for them.

The discovery of truth takes place in stages for human beings. It is the way all people learn, and the indirectness of the humor of analogy enables a man or woman to have the time that it takes to make the connections come together into the full meanings that need to be learned. We learn truth about God and about ourselves in ways that are unique to each of us and at different rates of speed, and therefore humorous analogy and parabolic story allows every learner to preserve their own unique learning curve. But through it all humor stands alongside as an encouraging reference point that is discovered incrementally throughout the journey of faith.

When I was a boy of about ten I clearly remember a large family dinner. My mother's favorite cousin who we affectionately called Uncle Erwin, though he was not our uncle, was a very funny man and was the source of many family jokes and stories that he told. At one particular dinner my mother had served everyone a piece of cake and there were exactly enough pieces for each person to have one piece. I was served my piece but to my disappointment it was an inside piece with frosting only on the top. I spoke out my complaint, "Mom, there are no sides with frosting on my piece." I had wanted an edge piece and I was looking toward my mother as I spoke my complaint. At just that minute, Uncle Erwin reached over with his fork and speared my whole piece of cake and put it in his mouth. I looked back and said even louder, "Hey where is my piece of cake?" Then Uncle Erwin smiled innocently, "O Earl, I'm sorry, I thought you said you didn't want your cake." At this point the whole family laughed at the hilarious way that Uncle Erwin had spoken his apology with his mouth full of cake. They also laughed at a lesson I had learned about the dangers of complaining in the Palmer family, especially if a humorist like Uncle Erwin happened to be near by. My mother was soft hearted and she managed to put together some frosting and cake fragments for her 10-year-old son but we had a humorous incident to add to our family's folklore from that day forward about the dangerous possibilities of complaining. Such family stories have a way of growing in sweetness and in joy as the years are added to our life journeys. Many youth who seem to be apparently oblivious to family occasions or important events as they happen in front of them will later in their young adult years recall in precise detail these stories and they will tell others how much they learned about life from those pastoral moments.

For this reason we need humorous events, occasions and memory-building traditions; traditions that become pastoral analogies along side of our experiences of life. These indirect signposts parallel our own life stories with markers that mean different things to us at different times. I remember one young man who had been active in the youth group at University Presbyterian Church Seattle where I started my career as a Presbyterian minister. He had been the vice-president of our youth fellowship and I was his youth pastor. But in his early college years he renounced his high school faith and described it as a phase he had once been involved in but had now had grown beyond. His public defection was a serious blow to our youth group and a very big disappointment to me personally and spiritually. Some ten years later I was the pastor at First Presbyterian Church of Berkeley and one Sunday at church here was this very man and his wife. He had by now received his Ph.D. in English literature and during those studies he had met the woman who became his wife. I will never forget what he said to me on that Sunday, "Earl, the very faith I once had contempt for I finally realized I could not live without." He had found again themes and stories and discoveries that were for awhile lost to him, but were now a part of who he really is and intends to be. The gospel of Jesus Christ turned out to be more durable than were his early college doubts. The loss of faith was the "phase"; the grace of God was the more durable reality. This is why the imagery of faith with its good humor and solemn memory and grateful hope, when it has been etched into the life story of a man or woman, is permanently there.

The long-term staying power of the Gospel should never be taken lightly, even when that man or woman seems to have forgotten.

Chapter Fourteen

The Humor of Love

Humor brings laughter and the best laughter of all comes from knowing that we are loved. The laughter of grace in the Bible is also the source of the best humor that we find throughout the Bible and throughout our life journeys too. It is the grand surprise of the discovery that I am beloved, that God cares about me, knows my name, and cares about my loved ones.

We meet this laughter in the first book of the Bible at a most terrifying moment in the life of Isaac, whose very name means "laughter." Isaac is the son of Abraham, and Abraham is told by God to offer Isaac, as a sacrifice at Mount Moriah (Gen 22). Abraham probably thought to himself as he and his son Isaac trudged up Mount Moriah carrying wood for an altar and fire for the sacrifice. "I knew it might finally come to this —that the God who called me out of Babylon would ask of me what all of the other gods ask." Abraham knows of the Molech practices of the ancient Babylonians and the Assyrians. It was a grim yet common ritual to offer child sacrifices to fertility gods. Abraham, trudging up Mount Moriah, is a typical religious man with his son along side doing a typical religious act—except for one thing: when Isaac asks his father, "Where is the sacrifice?" Abraham answers, "The Lord will provide." That one hope on Abraham's part, his trust in God's faithfulness, sets him apart from other religious men and women of his own time. The big event therefore on Mount Moriah was not Abraham's willingness to offer up as a sacrifice his son. Many people of his time and since then have done that. The big event is the interruption of Abraham by God. At just the right moment, God provided his own sacrifice. From that time forward, the only sacrifice Abraham or any man or woman after him need ever offer to God is the sacrifice of gratitude. Abraham and Isaac sacrifice a lamb that was caught in a thicket in place of Abraham's son, Isaac, and nothing will ever be the same again.

The big event at Moriah is the surprise of the grace of God. Abraham discovered that God loved his Son more than he did. Because of this holy interruption, Molech is totally rejected in the ritual of Israel. Throughout the Old Testament Molech is always called an abomination before the Lord. Ahab is described as the worst king of Israel and one of the chief reasons was that he practiced Molech according to the tradition of the Baal gods. The exciting and radical interruption on Mount Moriah gives the fullest meaning to Isaac's name. The two men may have walked slowly up the mountain, but they ran down the mountain. Something frightening and wonderfully good, even humorously good had happened to and for them so that the good news was now set loose in the world.

Each of the signs of the sheer grace of God in the Old Testament have profound surprise at their center. There is the solemn surprise in prophecies like Isaiah 53, "All we like sheep have gone astray and the Lord hath laid on him the iniquity of us all." These solemn texts tell of the costliness of grace. But there is also the good wonder of the sheer surprise. The purchase of the field at Anathoth by Jeremiah is funny; the pathetic complaint of Jonah about how good God is is also funny. Each of these has surprise at its core for all us who read these accounts.

The faithful protection by God of three young servants named Shadrach, Meshach and Abednego (Dan 3:25) is a frightening scene but also rich in humor. When the psalmist says, "I would rather be a doorkeeper in the house of the Lord than to dwell in the tents of wickedness" (Ps 84) we are struck with the humor in that contrast. We think to ourselves, "What kind of person would make such a choice? He or she must know something that a lot of people don't know. Most people would rather own tents wicked or not, than be doorkeepers."

In the New Testament the humor of grace also makes us laugh with the laughter of joy. The three parables that Jesus tells about lostness (Lk 15) describe four kinds of lostness in an unforgettable way. The lostness of illness with its disorientation in the case of the one sheep. The lostness of displacement about which the coin had no blame but nevertheless the coin was lost to its owner for a time. The lostness in the two sons was more complicated just as people are more complicated than sheep or coins. The one son is lost because of bad choices and the other son is lost because of self-righteous resentment.

But just as it happened at Mount Moriah, the best part of each of our Lord's lost and found parables is the finding and the celebration of joy when the finding happens. These are, in the deepest sense, parables about the housewife, the shepherd, and the father who finds and then hosts a great party because "the son who was lost is found, he was dead and is now alive." These parables are genuinely funny just as they are genuinely good because they have that living aroma of grace about them. There is humor in the parable of the Good Samaritan (Lk 10) for the same reason. The total surprise of it all, Jesus must be good at his core to think up such stories of salvation by surprise. The parable of the all day workers and the eleventh-hour workers last to be hired is also a humorous parable of grace even if the all day workers do not rejoice as much as they should at the discovery of how extravagantly generous their employer is.

The parable of the grand banquet to which street urchins are invited in from the highways and byways is funny just to imagine the incongruity of it all. What a strange dinner with such guests? Each one is a story about grace and each is humorous because Jesus has the sense of humor that goes with love.

Chapter Fifteen

The Humor of Joy

One question about humor always comes up from serious people. They ask a simple question: Why do we need humor in the first place? I have heard it put bluntly: "Let's just get on with the job, no need to humor us or tell us jokes." This question needs to be faced if we are to defend the humor of Jesus. Is Jesus "humoring" us needlessly when he tells parables, when he nicknames his disciples with names like "Rocky" for Simon son of John and "Sons of Thunder" for the two youngest disciples James and John, the sons of Zebedee? Someone could argue, "Aren't the simple traditional names good enough?" Also it can be argued, "Doesn't this humorous "new names" practice of Jesus just call more attention to the disciples than is spiritually healthy for them?" Will it not become a possible cause for the dangerous sin of pride? At an even more theologically important level we could ask if the true solemnity and costly grace of the sacrificial love of Jesus Christ is not compromised by humor.

Humor by its nature has the appearance of an "add on" that does not appear to be as vital to the same degree as other ingredients in any total context of reality. Why should fighting men and women who are at war be assembled for a U.S.O. show with Bob Hope and Jerry Calonna? Such entertainment is certainly not as essential for them as a long list of other ingredients such as food, proper equipment, training, the latest and best weapons, strategic planning, etc. This same question can be raised concerning such an event as the "water to wine" miracle in John 2. Where is the compassion in that sign since no one is healed of leprosy or blindness? Some could ask if it is even wise to do a miracle that does not appear to be socially responsible from the perspective of a court counselor who has been required to work with the problems of alcoholism and drunk driving. Why is it necessary for Jesus to walk on water in the middle of the night? Does this event have long term teaching significance? Parables pose their own special problem. Why a parable about a Samaritan and a wounded man? Why not simple, clear, direct teaching about what is the will of God concerning justice and public aid issues? The parable by its nature is subject to misunderstanding; therefore why would Jesus take such risks in his teaching ministry?

There are those who could argue that the use of humor has the same potential danger as parables in suggesting possible misunderstanding of the seriousness of our discipleship mandate. Humor has a softening effect as we have already observed; and it is logical to ask if that softening caused by laughter is a wise strategy for fighters in a war, or disciples on a mission to oppose the works of the darkness of this age. How does humor fit with the necessary sobriety and watchfulness that a disciple needs to exhibit in order to live out the apostolic mandate in the real world of persecution and evil?

These questions also go to the core of the purpose and meanings of humor. Is humor an add on, a nonessential ingredient that accompanies the reality core, or is it in some remarkable way a part of the mixture of the reality core itself?

This question about humor can be stated theologically as follows. Does *joy* as a great word of the Biblical discipleship experience have a ranking that can allow joy to stand along side *faith*, *hope* and *love*, the great three virtues of 1 Corinthians 13, "Now abide these three . . .?" How would the apostle Paul weight this fourth word *joy* and what does Jesus teach about the connection of joy with faith, hope and love? Is joy the non-essential but exciting add on to the greater and more important themes and experiences of faith, hope and love? No, joy is at the very core of God's reality scheme, just as laughter happens in heaven. St. Paul sees joy as the natural result of a faith, hope and love that is centered on Jesus Christ.

> We always give thanks to God for all of you and mention you in our prayers, constantly remembering before our God and Father your work of faith and labor of love and steadfastness of hope in our Lord Jesus Christ. For we know, brothers and sisters beloved by God, that he has chosen you, because our message of the gospel came to you not in word only, but also in power and in the Holy Spirit and with full conviction; just as you know what kind of persons we proved to be among you for your sake. And you became imitators of us and of the Lord, for in spite of persecution you received the word with joy inspired by the Holy Spirit . . .
>
> *(1 Thessalonians 1:2-6)*

I believe that the Old Testament portrayal of *hallel* (praise) in the Prophets and Psalmists is in full agreement with the New Testament portrayal of the word *chara* (joy). In both instances, the joy language is interpreted and portrayed as an essential part of love because love has a celebrative centerpoint and foundation that stands underneath and within its sacrificial costliness. That celebrative part of the core of love is the direct result of the extravagant nature of love. Jesus would tell a parable about two sons to make that joyous core ingredient unforgettable for us. "It is right that we celebrate and have a party . . ." These are not the words of the frivolous friends of a care-free youth who finally comes home from his wild trip to Europe. They certainly are not the words of the angry older brother who has kept track of his younger brother's immoral life. These are the words of the father as the one who suffered the humiliation, worry and grief of a boy who walked out and who is now home. The father, alone bears the cost of welcoming his son home, and it is the father who justifies the rightness of the celebration. It is he who invites his other son to join in with the joy and what is vitally important for that worried elder son is that the father assures this elder son of his own belovedness and safety with the very best promise of all: "Son, all that is mine is yours and you are always with me but this joy is right . . ." It is clear in this parable that our Lord has united joy with love so that the two cannot be separated from each other for very long.

Faith is the portrayal throughout the Bible of our trust in the faithfulness of God and it is this understanding of faith as trust in the trustworthiness and goodness of God that stretches throughout the whole of the Bible. This means that faith is not the skill that certain mystics have mastered nor is it a seven-step process of religious training. Faith trusts because faith wagers on the trustworthiness of the character of God. The joy in faith comes at that electric moment when a man or woman dares to trust in God and finds that this trust is validated in spite of the contradictions that were there early on during the time of deciding. How can the joy of the discovery of the faithfulness of God be eliminated from the core experience that the Bible calls faith in God? It is the joy that floods two lovers when a young man speaks the promise and commitment of love and then asks the woman he loves how she feels about his proposal. If she hugs him tightly and says "I love you, too, yes I want to marry you" then there is a joy that they experience together that surpasses even the strong sexual and emotional desires of attraction. The joy is the joy of faith; this joy is an essential part of the goodness of faith because faith in the one who deserves our trust is joyous just because it is so good and right. Jesus put it this way: "Take my yoke upon you for my yoke is easy and my burden is light." Jesus as a carpenter in his youth probably made wooden yokes for animals and therefore he knows all about their design. He assures us that he has made an easy yoke.

Hope is the assurance here and now that comes toward believers in the present but it comes from the future assurance that the God who we meet in our present journey of faith is the same one who reigns in the future. This assurance has the identical joy that is a part of love and faith because of the goodness of the one whom we will meet in that future.

Karl Barth explained the joy of this expectation clearly and simply: "There are no major surprises for a Christian believer when we die. We meet the same Jesus Christ at the end of history as we have come to know at the middle of history." Since it is Jesus Christ who we meet we have the best of all reasons to rejoice in our hope. Hope and joy cannot be separated from each other in the future expectations of a Christian as a Christian therefore looks out ahead.

The humor of Jesus is an ally of joy and therefore joy is not an extraneous add-on to greater realities. There are no greater realities. We are given permission to enjoy the rich humor of the Bible, but it is not only the humor that benefits from this good news about joy! Music benefits too! The celebrative and contemplative songs of faith are not luxuries for the rich; they have a secure home in Christian faith for the everyday ordinary Christian just as humor does. I believe that this place for music and the songs of faith has the same essential source of meaning in the Christian journey as does humor. There may be those of a serious frame of mind who do not agree. There are those who think that pipe organs and guitars, poets, dancers, actors, and singing groups should not take up so much space or time in the church of Jesus Christ. But these serious worriers and non-singers will need, in the words of Walt Hern (a poet and scientist) " to take a crash course to really fit in when they get to heaven if we are to believe the Bible's portrayals of heaven." Hell is the really serious future place to be because there is absolutely nothing to laugh, dance or sing about in that lonely place where, as C. S. Lewis put it, "each person is at an infinite distance from every other person." But Heaven will be the place of song and holy laughter (Rev 5; Lk 15).

We owe it to the next generation not only to hand on a legacy of social and human concern for justice, for love, for faithfulness, and for hope. We also owe the future generation a legacy of joy. That is where our collection of hymns and folk songs and poems fit in; it is where guitars of all kinds, drums, dance costumes, theatres and sports, peaceful times of human fellowship, all games for fun and the humorous stories we tell each in their own way have their place, too. It is one strong argument for the joy of beauty, and for the grand cathedrals that lift our eyes when we walk in to be surrounded by the stained glass portraits of God's faithful story. We humans instinctively begin to speak more softly when we enter a cathedral and that quiet joy of wonder should be a part, if possible, of every man and woman, girl or boys' experience. We owe it to them. This is why we owe it to the world and to the people of faith to keep real pipe organs and fine pianos in churches. The pipe organ is a marvelous instrument of pipes, reeds, chimes and wind and this most massive of all musical inventions was born in the church as the Christian church's grandest instrument of joy. It plays more softly than any other musical invention and when it is loud it is able to shake a building. We owe this instrument with its sense of wonder and sense of humor to the future generation. I remember attending a concert when I was a university student during which a large university choir and orchestra were presenting the marvelous American hymn *The Battle Hymn of the Republic*. During the final stanza an odd awareness began to overtake me of a profound underpinning that I began at first only to feel and then gradually more and more I became aware that a growing power and depth of deep bass notes were joining in with the chorus and orchestra. Then I saw it. In that concert hall the great pipe organ had entered the song; at first with such subtlety that it seemed as if flute and horn players a great distance away were gradually coming near to where we were. By the time the final notes of that hymn were sung with full choir and orchestra and full mighty pipe organ my heart had melted and tears were streaming down my face. It was the sheer joy of the good song of music sung to the glory of God. I want that joy for every girl and boy, young woman and young man, grandmother and grandfather. I want it to take them by surprise as it did me; I want them to be able to cry because it is so beautiful and well pleasing too. We are told that there will be such a day when the greatest chorale of all time shall be sung with a vast choir and you can be sure the pipe organs and the drums and the guitarists and the dancers and the poets and the ice skaters and the farmers and the scholars and the workers in factories and their children will be there doing what they do best to the glory of God. The song will be "Worthy is the Lamb" (Rev 5).

And we owe humor too. Humor is the story that joy tells. It was G. K. Chesterton who put it best of all: "I have often thought that the gigantic secret of God is his mirth." We humans need the mirth of Jesus not to be humored but to become more human which is one thing that humor does to and for and in us. The humor of joy draws us near to Jesus so that we want to trust him more. We owe this humor to our children because, however serious and heavy life is and can become, the greatest truth of all is this, that Jesus Christ who gave his life for our salvation is alive and therefore the word that pleases us more that all the other words is joy. St. Paul said it well in one of his most humorous lines, "Where sin increased the grace of God increased more." How is this possible? It is because of the Son of Man who began his ministry at the River Jordan along side of a very serious and earnest man called John the Baptist. John the Baptist was not a man given to humor and he must have been surprised by Jesus who wanted to be baptized by this serious prophet who called out the challenge of repentance. But then the best surprise of all came when God spoke. "This is my beloved son in whom I am well pleased."

CPSIA information can be obtained at www.ICGtesting.com
Printed in the USA
LVOW06s0450110813

347256LV00002B/666/A